AND JESUS SAID

AND JESUS SAID
The Parables of Jesus

WILLIAM BARCLAY

SAINT ANDREW PRESS
EDINBURGH

Originally published in 1952 by the
CHURCH OF SCOTLAND YOUTH COMMITTEE

Revised and published in 1970 by
SAINT ANDREW PRESS
121 George Street, Edinburgh EH2 4YN

Reprinted in 1971, 1972, 1975, 1980
Updated in 1992 by
SAINT ANDREW PRESS

ISBN 0 7152 0666 4

British Library in Cataloguing in Publication Data
A catalogue record of this book
is available from the British Library.

0-7152-0666 4

This book has been set in 11/12.5 pt Times.

Printed and bound by Bell and Bain Ltd., Glasgow

Contents

Acknowledgments

IN the Preface to the 1975 revised edition of this book, William Barclay acknowledged his indebtedness to the Revd Dr James Martin MA, BD for preparing the revision for press. The publisher of this edition would also like to express a similar gratitude for all Dr Martin's assistance over the years.

The publisher would also like to acknowledge the following:

The excerpt on p 63 from 'He was a Gambler too' by G A Studdert-Kennedy in *The Unutterable Beauty* (Mowbray: Oxford).

The excerpt on p 161 from 'The Creation' by James Weldon Johnson in *God's Trombones.*

The excerpt on p 171 from William Alexander: *Demonic Possession in the New Testament* (T&T Clark: Edinburgh).

The excerpt on p 196 from 'A Prayer' by John Drinkwater.

The scripture quotations used in this publication were taken from the Revised Standard Version and the Revised Version of the Apocrypha.

* denotes still in print at time of press.

Preface

by Ronald Barclay

LIKE so many of my father's early books, this volume, which was first published in 1952, was originally a Bible Class handbook. My father left Trinity Church, Renfrew in 1947 to take up his post as lecturer at the University of Glasgow, but all the things he learned in Renfrew never left him throughout his long university career. In the 1970 Preface to *And Jesus Said* my father talks of 'a simple uncomplicated book', and his experience with Bible Classes and young people during the formative years of his career left in him this desire to communicate in basic, simple language the truths and beliefs which make up our faith. The method my father uses is one which has stood the test of time:

(1) First of all, he goes into the background of the parable in some depth. This background knowledge helps us to understand the parable and what it must have meant to those who listened to Jesus telling it. What did Jesus mean to say at this or that particular moment? What must have been the effect of his word upon his hearers? My father used to say that his aim was to make the life and words of Jesus live against their contemporary background and, above all, to make them relevant for today.

(2) An interpretation of what the parable means follows this description of the background.

(3) Finally, there is usually a section on what the parable means for us today and what action we should take to follow Jesus' words. This final section is what gives *And Jesus Said* its unique message, as far as I am concerned. My father points us in a direct and challenging manner towards ways of thinking and behaving that might never have occurred to us. As he wrote at the end of the book, 'the Christian way demands an effort. But there is no joy like the joy of achievement; and we can be very sure that in the end the prize will be worth the

cost. "Be doers of the Word, and not hearers only" (James 1:22).'

For the reader coming to the parables for the first time this book will provide an excellent introduction. Although we might not class Jesus as a philosopher, the reader will find in the parables a whole system of general truths, and a firm basis for his or her faith which this book aims to uncover.

For someone who has come to delight in the parables and find much wisdom in them, *And Jesus Said* will provide new insights, fresh moments of inspiration and new hope. For all of us, young and old, the material in this book will offer a source of challenge, motivation, comfort and pleasure. 'In the recorded utterances of Jesus, nothing is so peculiar, so striking or so attractive as his parables. They stand alone. Nowhere else are there attributed to anyone parables that in number and beauty can be compared with those of the first three Gospels' (A T Cadoux: *The Parables of Jesus*). *And Jesus Said* will help you to come closer to Jesus and to an understanding of his message for today.

January 1992

'TO those
who by their constant encouragement
helped me
to write this book;
and to those
who by their constant criticism
saved this book from many errors
and myself from much pride.'

William Barclay

He taught them in Parables

The Immortal Stories

THERE are certain stories which are not so much the heritage of the scholar and the material of the theologian as the possession of every one of us; and such are the *parables* of Jesus. Even in an age when we know less and less of the Bible, and care less for it, it remains true that the stories Jesus told are the best known stories in the world.

The Method all Men knew

We must begin by asking, Why was it that Jesus used parables? Why was it that often, when he wished to open people's minds to some part of God's truth, he did so by telling them a story?

An answer may be found along the following lines of thought:

The first is *historical.* In all times in their history the Jews were familiar with teaching by means of parables. To make men and women see truth in such a way had always been a favourite method of their teachers. There are parables in the Old Testament. The most famous of them is in 2 Samuel 12:1-7. David coveted Bathsheba, the wife of Uriah, and in order to gain possession of her he deliberately arranged to have Uriah sent to his death (see 2 Samuel 11). For some time David was quite unaware that he had done anything wrong. So Nathan came to David and told him a simple story:

'There were two men,' said Nathan, 'who lived in a certain city. One was rich and had flocks and herds in abundance and all that his heart could desire. The other was a poor man who possessed one ewe lamb which was so dear to him that it was almost as one of his own family. A friend came to visit the rich man and he grudged to take of his own numerous flocks to set a meal before him; so he took and slaughtered the ewe lamb which was all that the poor man had ....'

David was a generous soul and at the story his heart kindled. 'Tell me who that man was. I swear that he will die for this and before he dies he will make restitution.'

Back came Nathan's answer like a bolt from the blue, '*You* are the man!'

That was a parable used to open a king's eyes. We can find another famous parable in Isaiah 5:1-7, the Parable of the Vineyard. So, when Jesus used parables he was using a method which, long before, the prophets had already and often most effectively employed.

Not only did the prophets use parables; the contemporary Rabbis, the great scholars and teachers of the day, also often used parables to get their lessons across. Here are some examples:

When Moses was feeding the sheep of his father-in-law in the wilderness, a young kid ran away; Moses followed it until it reached a ravine, where it found a well to drink from. When Moses got up to it, he said, 'I did not know that you ran away because you were thirsty. Now you must be weary.' He took the kid on his shoulders and carried it back. Then God said, 'Because you have shown pity in leading back one of a flock belonging to a man, you shall lead my flock Israel.'

Rabbi Pinchas ben Jair said: 'If thou seekest after the words of the Law as after treasures, God will not withhold from thee thy reward. It is like a man who lost a *sela*, or some other coin in his house, and lighted a lamp until he found it. If then a man kindles many lights seeking that which affords but an hour's pleasure in this world, until he finds it, how much rather shouldst thou dig for the words of the Law which assure thee of life in this world and the next, than for treasures.'

As we listen to the above story we can hear the voice of Jesus telling the story of the coin that was lost (see Luke 15:8-10).

Here is another older Jewish parable:
A king's son had fallen into evil ways. The king sent his instructor to him with the message, 'Come to thyself, my son.' But the son sent back this answer to his father: 'With what face can

I return? I am ashamed to come into thy presence.' Thereupon his father sent him word: 'My son, should a son be ashamed to return to his father? If thou returnest will it not be to thy father that thou comest?'

In the above we catch an echo of the Parable of the Prodigal Son (see Luke 15:11-32).

Elisha ben Abujah said:

'A man who does good works and who learns much Law, with whom is he to be compared? To a man who builds a house with stones for its foundation and bricks of clay above. Though the floods come and beat upon the side thereof, they cannot wash it away from its place. And a man who does not do good works and yet learns the Law, with whom is he to be compared? To a man who builds with bricks of clay first, and thereafter with stones. Even if but a little water flows it falls at once.'

Surely in this example is a glimpse of the Parable of the Wise and Foolish Builders (Matthew 7:24-27).

It was the greatness of Shakespeare that took the material of the historian Holinshed and created the immortal texture of Shakespeare's plays; it is the greatness of Jesus that took a common form of Jewish teaching and filled it with new meaning and beauty.

The Method all Men need

But Jesus used parables for other reasons, not only because they were an established form of teaching among his countrymen. For he was speaking in the first instance to Jews, and it was a characteristic of the Hebrew mind to be intensely *practical*. Oliver Cromwell once said to his troops, 'We speak *things*', meaning that he was not dealing with abstract ideas, but with concrete realities. That was of the very essence of the Jewish mind.

There was one basic difference between the Greek and Jewish mind. The Greek loved argument for argument's sake. Whether or not the argument ever reached any conclusion did not greatly matter. The Jew, on the other hand, was intensely interested in reaching conclusions; and, further, these conclusions had to be such that they led to action. The question of the Jewish mind was: *In view of all this, what must I do?* Because of this a story from real life, leading up to practical action, was the very thing that appealed to the Jewish mind.

But the parabolic method appeals to far more than the Jewish people. It has a well-nigh universal appeal for the ordinary person with the ordinary mind. Most of us tend to think in pictures; and most of us have difficulty in grasping abstract ideas. Philosophers can argue until doomsday about a definition of beauty or of goodness without reaching finality. But if we can point and say, 'that is a beautiful woman; that is a good man', then at once beauty and goodness become intelligible because they have become embodied in a person. If Jesus had argued from pure abstraction, using only ideas, few might have understood him. But he knew what was in mankind; and he gave us these cameo-like pictures we call *parables* so that the great ideas he wished to teach might become comprehensible.

This World and the Next

But there is yet another, fundamental reason why Jesus used parables. A *parable* has been defined as 'an earthly story with a heavenly meaning': Jesus used earthly things to lead our minds to heavenly things. As someone has said, 'He believed that there is no mere analogy but an inward affinity between the natural and the spiritual order.' Paul said something similar when he said that the visible world is designed to make known the invisible things of God (Romans 1:20).

For Jesus the whole wide world was the garment of the living God. Archbishop Temple said, 'Jesus taught men to see the operation of God in the regular and the normal—in the rising of the sun and the falling of the rain and the growth of the plant.' Sir Christopher Wren lies buried in St Paul's Cathedral, that great church which his own genius designed. On his tombstone is the simple inscription, '*If you want to see his monument, look about you.*' Jesus would have said that about God. He would have said: 'If you want to know what

4

God is like, look at the world. If you want to know what the Fatherhood of God is, look at human fatherhood at its finest and highest.'

This is important. There has always been a line of so-called Christian thought which despises this world as altogether evil. A Puritan was out walking with a friend. They passed a lovely flower by the wayside and the friend remarked upon its beauty. But the Puritan replied, 'I thank God I have learned to call nothing lovely in this lost and sinful world.' That was the precise opposite of the point of view of Jesus. His very use of parables shows that it was his conviction that the things of this world can lead our thoughts direct to God, *if we will only see*.

The Sudden Awakening

It has been pointed out that one of Jesus' greatest reasons for using parables was this—he wanted to persuade men and women to pass a judgment on things with which they were well acquainted, and then compel them to transfer that judgment to something to whose significance they had been erstwhile blind. That is exactly what Nathan did with David. He told him a story and David saw its meaning with crystal clarity. Then David passed a judgment on that meaning and situation. Nathan said, 'take that judgment and apply it to yourself.'

That was what Jesus did in his parables. He told a story with a meaning that was obvious to see, and the hearers could not help passing some kind of judgment even as the story was being told. Then Jesus demanded that they take that judgment and pass it on to something to which they had been erstwhile blind. If we apply that principle to almost any of the parables, we will see that they are sudden vivid flashes meant to make people see things which they were well able to see, but which either through deliberate blindness or through dullness of spirit, they had never truly *seen*.

The Master Craftsman

Here is another thing which we must bear in mind when we study the parables. We sit down and read a parable; we think it over; we probe and analyse it to bring out its inner message. We thrill to its interest, and often its sheer beauty touches our hearts. But it may be that we have never fully realised that *every one of Jesus' parables was produced on the spur of the moment.* They were not composed in the calm of the study where a man could sit and think up the story and polish the language like a lapidary polishing a jewel. They were produced instantaneously, in the cut and thrust of debate.

C J Cadoux said of the parables:

[They are] art harnessed for service and conflict .... [This is] why the parable is so rare. It requires a considerable degree of art, but art exercised under hard conditions. In the three typical parables of the Bible the speaker takes his life in his hands. Jotham (Judges 9:8-15) spoke his parable of the trees to the men of Sechem and then fled for his life. Nathan (2 Samuel 12:1-7) with the parable of the ewe lamb told an oriental despot of his sin. Jesus in the parable of the Wicked Husbandmen used his own death sentence as a weapon for his cause .... In its most characteristic use the parable is a weapon of controversy, not shaped like a sonnet in undisturbed concentration but improvised in conflict to meet the unpremeditated situation. In its highest use it shows the sensitiveness of the poet, the penetration, rapidity and resourcefulness of the protagonist and the courage that allows such a mind to work unimpeded by the turmoil and danger of mortal conflict.

Martin Luther said that Paul's Letter to the Galatians was 'like a sword flashing in some great swordsman's hand.' Like the parables, an insight into the sheer genius of the mind of Jesus. Remember that the parables are not carefully composed works of art, but sudden and lovely improvisations in the dust and heat of conflict. Quite apart from their religious value, they are supreme among the products of the mind of man.

The Principle of Interpretation

There is one final matter of general introduction before we set our-

6

selves to the interpretation of the individual parables. It is of primary importance to decide just *how* we are going to interpret them.

For a very long time it was almost universal custom to interpret them as *allegories.* An allegory is a story in which every person, event, detail has an inner meaning and stands for something else. The two most famous allegories in the English language are Bunyan's *Pilgrim's Progress,* and Spenser's *Faerie Queene.*

For example, C H Dodd quotes Augustine's interpretation of the parable of the Good Samaritan:

A certain man went down from Jerusalem to Jericho; Adam is meant; *Jerusalem* is the heavenly city of peace from the blessedness of which Adam fell; *Jericho* means the moon and signifies our mortality, because it is born, waxes, wanes and dies. *Thieves* are the devil and his angels, *who stripped him,* namely, of this immortality; *and beat him,* by persuading him to sin; *and left him half dead,* because in so far as man can understand and know God, he lives, but in so far as he is wasted and oppressed by sin, he is dead; he is therefore only *half dead.* The *Priest* and *Levite* who saw him and passed by signify the priesthood and ministry of the Old Testament, which could profit nothing for salvation. *Samaritan* (in Hebrew) could mean Guardian, and therefore the Lord himself is signified by this name. *The binding of the wounds* is the restraint of sin. *Oil* is the comfort of a good hope; *wine*, the exhortation to work with fervent spirit. The *beast* is the flesh in which Jesus designed to come to us. The being *set upon the beast* is belief in the incarnation of Christ. The *inn* is the Church where travellers are refreshed on their return from pilgrimage to their heavenly country. The *morrow* is after the resurrection of the Lord. The *two pence* are either the two precepts of love, or the promise of this life and of that which is to come, or, possibly, the two sacraments. The *innkeeper* is the apostle Paul. The promise he makes to pay any extra expenses incurred is either his counsel of celibacy or the fact that he worked with his own hands lest he be a burden to any of the brethren.

Well, one thing is quite clear about an interpretation like the above. No one on earth could produce it unless he or she sat down and worked at the parable for hours and days together. For that reason it is obviously the *wrong* interpretation. We have to remember two things. First, the parables were weapons of controversy, struck off in the heat of the moment. Second, in the first instance they were always *spoken* to an audience, always *heard* by a body of listeners, not read. And mostly they would be heard *once*, as a sermon is heard. No one listening to a thing for the first time could ever make the necessary mental transpositions to produce an interpretation like that. The parable is essentially a sword to stab men's minds awake; and therefore its interpretation can never be that which could be discovered only after long labour in the study. It must be one single truth which the story illuminates which leaps out to meet the listener's mind.

Two Things to Remember

If that be so, two things stand out. First, to understand any parable properly we need to have a knowledge of the circumstances in which it was spoken. In many cases we have that, and so the parable must always be interpreted in the light of this background. Sometimes we do not possess that background and must try to reconstruct it; but when we do possess it, it must dominate our interpretation. Second (and we will do well *always* to remember this), it is obviously impossible to find the whole of the Christian faith in any one parable. The parable was originally spoken by Jesus to illustrate one aspect of truth, to stress that particular aspect which the need of the moment required. For example, it is wrong to find the whole of Christian theology in the Parable of the Prodigal Son and to forget that there are parables of judgment and *vice-versa*. But if we remember that the situation in which a parable was spoken will always shed light on its meaning, and that in every case Jesus is throwing into bold relief one aspect of the truth, then when we put the parables all together we shall gain an unmatched insight into the mind of the Master Teacher.

2

The Sower and the Seed
Matthew 13:1-9; Mark 4:1-9; Luke 8:4-8

The First of the Parables

ACCORDING to Matthew's narrative this is the first parable Jesus ever spoke. In Palestine it was the custom for crowds to follow famous Rabbis wherever they went so that they could catch the pearls of wisdom which fell from the teachers' lips as they walked. Jesus was walking by the seaside, and such a throng of people wished to hear him that he was nearly pushed into the sea. To escape the press of the crowd Jesus embarked on a boat. In the boat he sat down to speak to the people, for teachers, in those days, sat to teach. It may well be that in this case Jesus was describing something that was actually happening as he was speaking, and that at that very moment he could see the sower sowing in the fields up from the seashore.

The Different Kinds of Ground

In the parable four different kinds of ground are mentioned.

(1) There was the *wayside ground*. In Palestine the common ground was divided into long narrow strips which each man could cultivate as he wished. There was no fence or wall round the strips, but between each of them ran a narrow ribbon of ground perhaps not much more than three feet across. These narrow dividing ribbons were rights of way. Anyone could walk up and down them. The result was that they were beaten as hard as a pavement by the feet of countless passers-by. When any seed fell on them it might as well have fallen on the road for all the chance it had of getting into the ground.

(2) There was the *rocky ground*. This does not mean ground that was full of stones. In Palestine there were many places where there was only a skin of earth over a shelf of limestone rock. The rocky ground was ground like that. It had no depth. If the seed fell there it would

sprout quickly; but the moisture and the nourishment it needed to withstand the heat of the sun were simply not there and it soon withered and died.

(3) There was the *thorny ground*. At the moment that ground would look good enough. It is easy to make a garden look clean by simply turning over the soil. But if the weeds have been allowed to go to seed the seeds are still there in the earth and it is proverbial that one year's seeds make seven years' weeds. So in that ground the seeds of the weeds were still there; and there was only one possible result—the good seed had the life choked out of it.

(4) There was the *good ground*. It was receptive enough to take the seed in; it had depth to allow the seed to let down its roots and draw the nourishment and the moisture it needed; it was clean enough to give the seed an unhindered chance to grow.

In any field in Palestine a man would find these different kinds of soil; everyone would recognise at once the picture Jesus drew.

The Word of God and the Mind of Man

There are two main interpretations of this parable.

We begin with what we may call the traditional interpretation. At its widest, that interpretation says that the parable means that the word of God is always good, but that the outcome of it depends on the heart and the mind into which it falls. On this interpretation the different kinds of ground stand for different states of the hearts and minds of men.

(1) There is the wayside ground. This stands for the shut mind. We sometimes say of a person, 'We might as well talk to a brick wall as to him.' His mind is shut and the truth cannot gain entry. There are many cases of this shut mind.

(a) There is *mental laziness*. Some people are so lazy that they refuse to think. Socrates found this. He wanted to make men think, and so he went about the streets of Athens with his disturbing questions until men thought of him as a kind of gad-fly; and because they did not want to think, they in the end sentenced him to death.

Alfred Lord Tennyson, in his poem 'The Lotus Eaters', tells over again the story of the sailors of Ulysses who came to the island where the Lotus flower grew. Whoever ate of that flower never again wished to make any effort, but desired only to lie and sleep in that land where it was always afternoon. So the sailors who had eaten of it sang:

Let us alone. What pleasures can we have
To war with evil? Is there any peace
In ever climbing up the climbing wave?
Give us long rest or death, dark death, or dreamful ease.

They finish their song:

Surely, surely slumber is more sweet than toil, the shore
Than labour in the deep mid-ocean, wind and wave and oar;
Oh rest ye, brother mariners, we will not wander more.

All they wanted was to be left alone. In the book of Hosea there is one of the most terrible of all condemnations—'Ephraim is joined to idols; let him alone' (Hosea 4:17). There can come a stage in mental laziness when a person's mind is shut. But we are thinking creatures and not to think is to shut the mind to God's truth.

(b) There is *mental arrogance*. There is the attitude of the man who thinks he knows everything already, and that he has nothing left to learn. That was the attitude of the Pharisees to Jesus. They did not want to know anything that Jesus had to say because they thought they know it all already. This is the spirit which begets intolerance and which shuts the mind to truth. Oliver Cromwell, writing to the intolerant Scots of the day, said, 'I beseech you by the bowels of Christ think it possible that you may be mistaken.' There are many way to God; and no one should shut his mind to every way but his own.

(c) There is *mental fear*. Another way to put this is to call it wishful thinking. It is quite possible for a person to shut his mind, either consciously or unconsciously, to what he does not wish to be true. The Psalmist (Psalm 53:1) says, 'The fool says in his heart, "There is no God".' The word used for *fool* does not mean a man with no brains; it means a man who is a fool in the moral sense of the term. He denies the existence of God, not because he is intellectually convinced that God does not exist, but because *he does not want God to exist*. The Scots proverb says, 'There's none so blind as winna see.'

(2) There is the rocky ground. This stands for those whose faith is shallow. In Christianity it is always necessary to think things out and to think things through. Dr J Alexander Findlay once said, 'It is not easy to be a Christian; but it is easy to start.' It is not difficult to have our feelings affected in such a way that we are deeply moved and attracted by Christ. But unless we go on to think things out and think them through, whenever some storm comes, or when difficulties arise, faith is likely to collapse.

Jesus was always telling men to count the cost of following him. The whole of the tenth chapter of Matthew is one long summons to be sure what it means to be a disciple. When a man wished to become a member of the Benedictine order of monks, the Benedictines took him in and gave him his cell and the teaching and training that he required. But for one whole year they left the clothes he had worn in the world in his cell. At any time he was free to take these clothes, put them on again and walk out. Only after a year did they take his clothes away and leave him with nothing but his monk's habit. They wished to make quite sure that the man had counted the cost and knew what he was doing.

To be a sure faith, the Christian's faith must be deeply rooted.

(3) There is the thorny ground. This stands for the life so crowded with other things that Christ gets crowded out. The best commentary on that is a kind of parable which a nameless prophet told to King Ahab. He told how during a battle he had been left in charge of a prisoner, with the warning that if the prisoner escaped his own life would be forfeit. But he allowed his attention to be distracted and the prisoner escaped; his excuse was, 'As your servant was busy here and there, he was gone' (1 Kings 20:38-40).

It is possible to be so busy living that we do not think *how* we are living. It is possible to be so busy doing things that we forget the necessity of prayer and quietness and devotion and study. And it is by no means always things which are bad in themselves which crowd out the most important things. It has been said that the second best is the worst enemy of the best. This is a warning that life must not be so full of other interests that the main interest is neglected.

(4) There is the good ground. In each of the three accounts there is attached an interpretation of this parable. Scholars are sure that this is not the actual words of Jesus, but rather the interpretation that the Church put upon the parable. However that may be, if we put the three interpretations together, we get a picture of the ideal listener.

(a) Matthew 13:23 says that the good listener *understands* the word. That is to say, he does not merely listen, he bends his mind to ask, *What does this mean?* It is always a good rule about any bit of truth to say, *I will not stop thinking about this until I discover what it really means.*

(b) Mark 4:4-20 says that the good listener *accepts* the word. That means that he takes it right into his mind. We often say of a bad listener that he or she lets things go in one ear and out the other. To accept a thing into our minds means that we really possess it, that it has become part and parcel of our thought and life.

(c) Luke 8:15 says that the good listener *holds* the word fast. That means that he accepts the truth in such a way that he obeys it under all circumstances; it is not something upon which he acts when it is convenient and discards when it is inconvenient.

So then, on this traditional interpretation, the parable means that if we bend our minds to find the meaning of the word of God, if we accept it in such a way that it becomes part and parcel of our very being, if we hold fast to it at all times and in all places, it will enable our lives to bring forth wonderful fruits.

The Necessary Risk

But there is a more modern interpretation. On this second view the parable is spoken mainly to the disciples, to meet their growing disillusionment and discouragement. To them Jesus was the most wonderful person in the world, who spoke with a wisdom and an authority they had never heard before. And yet, in spite of that, he was being met with growing hostility; and it was clear that a great deal of his preaching was going for nothing. So, it is suggested, Jesus spoke this parable mainly to meet the spoken or the unspoken question of his disciples, 'Master, why does so much effort produce so little result?' The meaning of the parable then becomes, *No matter how much seed may seem to be wasted, in the end a great harvest is sure.* The point of the parable in this case lies entirely in the one verse, Matthew 13:8. Now there is a great truth here. It is true that no farmer would refuse to sow his seed just because he knows that some of it will be wasted. He knows that even if some of the seeds never grow, nonetheless a harvest will result. From this interpretation two great lessons emerge.

(1) We must never be discouraged even when nothing seems to be happening. Just before 1640 a young man called John Harvard emigrated from England to America; he was one of the most brilliant scholars in this country; and all predicted the brightest future for him. In America he lived for only one year and then he died. When he died he left a little over £700 and a collection of more than 200 books to a new university in America. That university became the renowned Harvard University. The death of John Harvard perhaps looked like waste, but it produced an abundant harvest. So then this parable teaches that even if much effort seems to go for nothing, the harvest is sure.

(2) We must be prepared to take a risk. Every time the farmer sows he takes a risk, for so many things can interfere with the harvest. In the book of Ecclesiastes there is a fine verse on this essential risk. 'He who observes the wind will not sow; and he who regards the clouds will not reap' (Ecclesiastes 11:4). It is quite true that if we wait for perfect conditions we will never act at all. When John Logie Baird was experimenting with television, all the equipment he could afford was old biscuit tins and reels of thread and the like. When Abraham Lincoln wished to learn to read and write, all the materials he had were a wooden shovel which he scraped white for an exercise book and a bit of burnt stick for a pencil. So then this parable would say to us: *Start with what you have: don't wait for perfect conditions; risk everything for what you believe to be right, and surely in the end the harvest will come.*

3

The Kingdom of God is at Hand

The Kingdom

AS we study the parables we come across again and again the phrase *the Kingdom of God*. So often does it occur, and so important is this conception, that it is best to treat it in a chapter all by itself.

The Chosen People

From the beginning of their history the people of Israel held the conviction that they were in some unique sense the people of God; so much so that there was a line of thought which considered that the desire for an earthly king of any kind was an insult to God. After Gideon's mighty exploits the people came to him and asked him to be king and to found a royal dynasty. His answer was, 'I will not rule over you, and my son will not rule over you; the Lord will rule over you' (Judges 8:23). There we have the conviction that the kingship belongs to God and cannot be given to any man. When the people came to Samuel asking him to give them a king, he was displeased; and when he took counsel with God, God said to him, 'They have not rejected you, they have rejected me from being king over them' (1 Samuel 8:6,7). There again is the conviction that Israel could have no other king but God. That particular conception did not last, but the idea that they were the chosen people was ineradicably fixed in the minds of the people of Israel.

The World Empire

Generally speaking the dream the Israelites had was that because they were the chosen people, they were destined for world dominion. It often happens that a nation has some great period in its history to which it looks back as the golden age. To Israel that time was the time of

David; and they looked forward to the day when some great king of the Davidic line would sit upon the throne again and lead them to greatness. So Isaiah 11:1 looks forward to the coming of 'a shoot from the stump of Jesse.' In the great vision of Isaiah 9:2-7 it is the throne of David which is to be established without end. In Jeremiah 30:9 the dream is that in the great days to come they will serve the Lord their God and David their king 'whom I will raise up for them' (*cf* Jeremiah 22:4; 23:5; 33:22).

At that time different prophets had different ideas of what was to happen to the Gentiles, the non-Jewish peoples. Sometimes it was held that the Gentiles would come seeking out Israel and asking to be taught the true way. So in Isaiah 2:2 we have the picture of the Gentiles flowing to the mountain of the Lord to be taught about the true God. Still more often the idea was that the Gentiles would be absolutely subdued. If they were not destroyed they would become at best the slaves of Israel. So Isaiah 45:14 has the vision of the Gentiles coming in chains; and Isaiah 60:12 says bluntly and almost savagely, 'For the nation and kingdom that will not serve, you shall perish; those nations shall be utterly laid waste.' Here is the dream of world dominion at its most vivid. Rarely, very rarely, there is the idea, not that the Gentiles should come humbly seeking Israel, but that Israel should go out as the missionary of God to seek the Gentiles and bring to them the one true light. So Isaiah 49:6 tells of God saying, 'I will give you as a light to the nations, that my salvation may reach to the ends of the earth.' But human nature being as it is, it was the hope of world dominion upon which the Jews nourished their hearts.

The National Disaster

At its best and its biggest Palestine was always a little land. But there entered into Jewish history a series of disasters.

First of all the kingdom was split in two never to be reunited again. At the death of Solomon about 900 BC, ten of the twelve tribes went off under Jeroboam and only two remained faithful to Rehoboam who had foolishly threatened them with heavier burdens than any his father had imposed on them. The history of that split is in 1 Kings 12. So now there were two little kingdoms, the northern kingdom of Israel with its capital at Samaria, and the southern kingdom of Judah with its capital at Jerusalem. World empire seemed further away.

But the disasters were not finished. Round about 725 BC the Assyrians invaded and conquered the northern kingdom. In those days conquerors often followed the extremely cruel practice of removing the native population to some other land and settling strangers in the new empty land. Those Israelites who were removed are the lost ten tribes, for they vanished completely from history.

Less than two hundred years later disaster smote the southern kingdom. Around the year 585 BC the Babylonians invaded Judah and the same disastrous fate fell upon the southern kingdom as the northern. But there was one vital difference. The people of Judah were taken away to Babylon, but they stubbornly refused to lose their identity. Jews they were, and Jews in spite of everything they remained.

So another century and a half passed and about the year 440 BC the Jews, still clinging to their nationality, were allowed to return to Jerusalem under Ezra and Nehemiah and to rebuild as best they could their shattered city and their devastated Temple. And amazingly, one of the miracles of history, is that they had not lost their dream. They were still in their own eyes God's chosen people. Their history might be one long series of disasters, but they were quite certain that their great day would still dawn. History has no greater example in all the world of faith like that. From that day forward the Jews had little freedom. They were subject in turn to the Babylonians, the Persians, the Greeks and the Romans; but with unconquerable tenacity they hugged their dream to their hearts. Happen what may, they were the chosen people and greatness was their destiny.

The Intervention of God

But now the dream began to change. In the old days, when they were still a nation, they looked to greatness through the work of some son of David. That hope never completely died, for it was *Son of David* that the crowds called Jesus as he rode into Jerusalem. But there came a vital alteration into it. It was plain that by human means the Jews were most unlikely ever to achieve greatness; and so they began to dream of a day when God would break directly into history and that destiny which could not be achieved by natural means would be achieved by supernatural power.

The Two Ages

Into this scheme of things entered another dominating idea. From now, to the Jew, all history fell into two ages. There was the present age which was altogether bad and lost; and there was the age to come which would be the age of vindication, of glory and of God. But in between the two ages there was to come that day which haunts the pages of the Old and New Testaments, *The Day of the Lord*. It would come without warning. It would be a day of world upheaval and of judgment. There are terrible descriptions of it in Isaiah 2:12ff; Jeremiah 30:7ff; Joel 2; Amos 5:20. So now we have the Jews sunk in material and national disaster, still clutching to themselves the undefeatable hope and waiting for the sudden breaking of the Day of the Lord which would be the birth pangs of the glorious age to come.

The Son of Man

Now there enters into this Jewish world of thought another conception of fundamental importance for the New Testament in general and for the understanding of some of the parables. It is the idea of *the Son of Man*. That title goes back to the book of Daniel. In Daniel 7:1-14 the seer has a vision of the terrible empires which had up to this time possessed world power and dominated the Jews. Each of these he sees under the form of a wild beast. The first (7:4) is like a lion with eagles' wings. This stands for the Babylonian Empire. The second is like a bear with three ribs in its mouth as if it was devouring the carcass (7:5). This stands for the empire of the Medes. The third is like a leopard with four wings and four heads (7:6). This stands for the Persian Empire. The fourth is a namelessly terrible beast with iron teeth and ten horns (7:7). This stands for the Macedonian Empire. In turn each of these beasts had held the dominion but now it is taken from them. And then there comes one like unto a son of man (7:13, 14) and the dominion is given to him.

The Authorised Version needlessly complicated matters by saying that this figure was like *The* Son of Man and introducing capital letters. The real meaning of the passage is this. Up to now, world power has been held by empires which were so bestial that they could be typified only by savage animals; now it is to be given to the saints of the Most High (7:18), to a power kindly, gracious, humane, which can be typified only by a human figure in opposition to the savage beastliness which went before. Originally in Daniel the figure of a son of man was not a person, but a symbol of gentleness in contradistinction to the terrible powers which had gone before.

Between the Testaments

Between the Testaments is was easy to personify this son of man into *The Son of Man,* the almighty deliverer promised by God. In that period, especially in the book of Enoch, which Jesus must have known and read, the Son of Man comes to stand for a figure waiting in heaven until the appointed hour when he will suddenly descend to earth, sweep away every hostile power and complete at last the long dream of the Jews.

The Idea of Jesus

It was into such a background that Jesus came. He knew all this. We can be quite certain that Jesus never thought of the Kingdom of God in terms of worldly empire. Yet he did use this phrase and he did call himself *Son of Man,* thereby showing that he did regard himself as God's chosen instrument in the bringing of his kingdom.

What did Jesus mean when he spoke of the Kingdom of God? Well, we must clarify one thing straight away. The word *kingdom* here is an abstract noun. It does not mean an area of land as we speak of the Kingdom of Britain or Belgium or Holland. It does not means the domain, but *the dominion* of God. We can see then that the Kingdom of God does not mean a territory in which God is king; it means a condition of the heart and mind and will—where God is Lord of all.

Past, Present and Future

In Jesus' teaching about the Kingdom there is one paradoxical set of facts. He speaks of the Kingdom as being three things all at the one time.

(1) Sometimes he says that the Kingdom has existed in the *past.* In Luke 13:28 he speaks of Abraham, Isaac and Jacob and all the prophets in the Kingdom of God. If the patriarchs and the prophets are in the Kingdom then it has long existed.

(2) He speaks of the Kingdom as *present.* In Luke 17:21 he says either 'The Kingdom is in the midst of you', or perhaps 'The Kingdom is within you.' In Luke 11:20, speaking of his own miraculous cures, he says, 'If it is by the finger of God that I cast out demons, then the Kingdom of God has come upon you.' The Kingdom is here and now.

(3) Often he speaks of the Kingdom as *future.* In Luke 12:32 he tells his disciples that it is God's good pleasure to give them the Kingdom, clearly at some time to come.

How can the Kingdom be past, present and future all at the one time? We find our key in the Lord's Prayer. In it (Matthew 6:10) two petitions come side by side: *Thy kingdom come. Thy will be done, on earth as it is in heaven.* Now the Jews had a habit of saying things in two different forms side by side. Almost any verse of the Psalms will demonstrate that. So then these two phrases in the Lord's Prayer, as it were, explain each other. If that is so *the Kingdom of God is a society on earth where God's will is as perfectly done as it is in heaven.* That is why the Kingdom can be past and present and future. Any one in any age and generation who has perfectly done God's will was in the Kingdom; those who do God's will are in the Kingdom; but the final consummation when the whole world will do God's will is something which is still to come.

So when Jesus spoke of the Kingdom of God he thought of doing God's will as perfectly on earth as it was done in heaven. He himself always did that, not just sometimes as others had done, but always.

That is why the Kingdom perfectly begins with him. He thought of how happy everyone would be if only they did that; of what a wonderful world this would be if it was ruled by God's will; of how God's heart would be glad when men and women did perfectly accept his will. Truly when that happened there would be heaven on earth. That is why for Jesus *the Kingdom* was the most important thing of all. And that is why for so long no one understood him. When they spoke of the Kingdom they were still thinking of the old nationalistic dreams of world power and they would have liked to make him a king like that. But he was thinking of doing the will of God and it was in their hearts, and not on their earthly thrones, that he wished to reign.

4

So is the Kingdom of God
Mark 4:26-29

A Parable of Patience

THIS parable also has a traditional and modern interpretation. Let us begin with the traditional one, that it is a parable of patience. In this direction it has two lines of meaning.

(1) The first springs directly from the circumstances in which Jesus was speaking. We have seen (chapter 3) how the Jews clung to the idea that sooner or later God would vindicate them and their great day would come. Now there were many who desired to hasten that day and clamoured for swift and violent action. In Jesus' time rebellion was in the air. This parable tells the hot-heads that the way of violence is not God's way, that God's plans are working themselves out and that too much haste, instead of helping them on, keeps them back.

(2) The second is a universal meaning. It is a warning to all who are in too big a hurry. It is characteristic of our modern outlook that we want quick results. A traveller tells how he paid many visits to the United States of America. On his first visit he came to the conclusion that the great desire of the Americans was for *power*. On his second visit, he formed the opinion that the great desire of the Americans was for *money*. But on his third visit he formed the opinion that the great desire of the Americans was for *speed*; and that impression remained with him. What they wanted above all was to gain faster and faster results.

That is precisely the temptation which Jesus himself had to face. From one point of view that was the whole impact of his temptations at the beginning of his ministry. At that time he had to make a great and far-reaching decision; he had to decide what methods to use in order to win men for his cause.

The first temptation was to turn stones into bread. The little limestone rocks of the desert were exactly like little loaves. The tempter said to him, 'You want men? Go on then, give them bread and they will pour after you in hordes.' But Jesus said, 'No; man does not live by bread alone but by every word that comes from God.' He would not use methods that by a kind of bribery would produce quick results which would fade just as quickly.

The next temptation was to leap from the temple pinnacle and float down unharmed. That was the temptation to use sensations. 'You want quick results?' said the tempter. 'Well then, unleash a few really startling miracles. That will send them scurrying after you.' But again Jesus said, 'No; I cannot play tricks with God's power like that.' He knew quite well that a thing can be a nine days' wonder and then forgotten.

The last temptation was to worship Satan. That was the temptation to compromise. 'You want your results?' said the tempter. 'Well, just compromise with evil a little. Strike a bargain with me. Don't be so unbending in your demands. Give in a little to the world and you will be the most popular figure in Palestine.' Again Jesus said, 'No; right is right and wrong is wrong and there can be no compromise.' He would have nothing to do with a policy which produced quick but impermanent results.

There are times when there is nothing to do but wait. Once a fracture has been set in plaster, or a wound bandaged, the process of healing must take its own time. Once a seed has been planted, the process of growth must be allowed to go on at its own pace. This parable teaches patience.

The Gradual Growth

It also teaches that the growth of the Kingdom is a gradual growth. In the growth of the corn there are the necessary stages: first the blade, then the ear, then the full corn ripe in the ear. Unless these necessary stages are gone through nothing can happen.

That is a universal law of life. No one ever learned a language overnight. No one ever woke up in the morning a mathematician. No one ever became a great musician in the flash of an eye. All great things come gradually.

23

Someone tells of a scientist who used an experiment to prove this. He had a very large beaker of pure clear water and a very little phial of dye. He dropped one drop of the dye into the water and there appeared to be no change whatever. Another, then another drop, but for a long time the water still appeared quite clear. And then suddenly, as a drop went in, the whole beaker began to tint. It was the steady persistence of the dropping that made it happen.

If we are learning we must remember that knowledge never comes in a hurry, but that it must be gained step by step. If we are teaching we must remember that effects rarely come quickly, but that slowly and gradually the mind opens to the light and the heart of God. This is the parable to read in time of discouragement.

The Kingdom is God's

This parable also teaches that at the back of things there is God. It is a parable to put us in our proper place. In the parable it is said that the earth makes things grow of herself. No one can make anything grow. The scientist can make a synthetic seed. If it is analysed it will have in it all the elements of a natural seed; but there is just one difference—*it will not grow*. There are certain things that only God can do. In the last analysis it is not man who brings in the Kingdom, but God who gives it.

Clearly there is danger in over-stressing this truth. Karl Barth, for instance, in his address to the World Council of the Churches in Amsterdam in 1948, spoke the following:

'We must free ourselves from all quantitative thinking, all statistics, all observable consequences, all efforts to achieve a world Christian order .... We are not the ones to change this world into a good one. God has not resigned his lordship over it into our hands. The salvation of the world which has already been accomplished is not our work. And so will that which still remains, the revealing of the world's salvation in a new heaven and a new earth, not be our work but his.'

Here is the point of view that man himself can do nothing and that God must do *everything*. Someone poked fun at this in a parody of a well-known hymn:

Sit down, O men of God,
  His Kingdom he will bring,
Whenever it may please his will;
  You cannot do a thing.

There is truth in that point of view, but there is error too. It is true that no man can make a seed grow, but it is also true that *man can see to it that conditions exist in which the seed has a chance to grow.* It is true that man cannot bring in the Kingdom; that God must in the end bring it in; but it is also true that today millions of people are living under conditions where the seed of the word has hardly a chance to grow. A story was told of a woman who was taken from a slum tenement for a day in the country. As she saw the green grass and the sky and the blue of the sea, she said wistfully, 'It would be so much easier to be good in a place like this.' The fact that God alone can bring in the Kingdom does not absolve us from the serious duty of seeking with all our strength to produce conditions in which the seed of God's words and the moving of God's Spirit will have their finest chance to work.

There is a crowded part of a certain great city where at one time every seventeenth house was a pub. There are people living in conditions where common decency, let alone morality, is very difficult. The Christian cannot say, 'Let God mend it.' In the old days two Scotsmen, Lord Rea and Lord Ramsay, were talking of how bad things were. One said to the other, 'Well, God mend all.' 'Faith,' flashed back the other, 'we maun *help* him to mend it.' In other words, it is our Christian duty to be fellow-labourers with God.

The Christian Confidence

But in the end this is a parable of confidence. It tells us that the process may be slow but it is sure. A preacher, speaking about the occasion when Uzzah stretched out his hand to steady the Ark of God and was stricken dead for his temerity, said that it was a warning to all those 'who were filled with an irreligious solicitude for God.' This parable tells us not to worry.

There is nothing so unstoppable as the power of growth. We have all seen the way a tree can crack a concrete pavement with its power. In London during the war there was a church prepared for harvest festival Sunday. On the Saturday the first of the great blitzes came: that harvest festival was never held because the church lay in ruins. But on the table there had been sheaves of corn. The autumn passed and the winter. The spring came and there was a bombsite with little green shoots all over it. The summer passed and the autumn came again, and on that bombsite there was a flourishing patch of corn. Not even the fire and the bombs could keep the corn from sowing its seeds and growing.

The Time of Harvest is come

There is another and more modern interpretation of this parable. It finds the whole point in verse 29 and especially in the last phrase— *the harvest has come*. With Jesus something absolutely new had come into the world. He was the embodiment of the Kingdom because his whole life was lived in complete accordance with the will of God. Confronted with that life, people either loved or hated him and their reaction to him was their own judgment. The harvest had come.

Love and Judgment

In the Fourth Gospel there is a strange paradox. The great text in John 3:16 says that 'God so *loved* the world that he gave his only Son.' Then the gospel goes on, 'God sent the Son into the world, not to condemn the world, but that the world might be saved through him.' In John 12:47 Jesus says, 'I did not come to judge the world but to save the world.' But in this very same gospel Jesus says, 'For judgment I came into this world' (9:39). 'The Father judges no one, but has given all judgment to the Son' (5:22).

Here indeed is a paradox; and yet there is no mystery-mongering. It is often possible to offer an individual something in sheer love and for that something yet to be a judgment on that person. Suppose we are very fond of great drama or great music. We have a friend with whom we wish to share these precious things. We take him to a great play or to hear a famous orchestra. He fidgets and is obviously bored. He had passed a judgment on himself. It was sheer affection which prompted us to offer him this experience; it was given in love and yet it was a judgment.

So God sent his son into the world because he loved the world; but if a man's reaction to Christ is lack of interest or hostility, that man has judged himself. The gift of God's love which was meant to save him has in the end condemned him. The parable, in this view, would teach that the harvest has come because a man by his reaction to Jesus has either included himself with God or excluded himself from God.

5

An Enemy hath done this
Matthew 13:24-30

A True Story

THIS is usually called the Parable of the Wheat and the Tares. The *tares* were a weed called 'bearded darnel' which in its early stages was so like wheat that it was next to impossible to distinguish them. In fact before the head appeared, not even the wisest farmer could tell one from the other. After that, the difference was clear; but by that time, the roots had become so inextricably intertwined that any attempt to root out the darnel would have torn out the wheat too.

There were three ways in which the darnel could be separated from the wheat. (a) The darnel in the end did not grow so high as the wheat: in a badly-infested field sometimes the wheat was reaped over the top of the darnel and then the whole field set on fire and the darnel burned out. (b) Quite often as the reaper reaped he separated the wheat from the darnel, dropping the darnel in bundles behind him so that afterwards it could be collected and burned. Or (c) sometimes in a case where there was just a little darnel in a field, the seed was picked out from the good wheat before the grain was milled. This was women's work. The wheat and the darnel grain were exactly the same size but they were easily distinguished because the darnel was slate grey in colour. This had to be done because the darnel was semi-poisonous and would have had very harmful consequences had it been allowed to remain mixed with the wheat.

This parable is not a highly improbable story made up by Jesus to enforce a moral lesson. It is the kind of thing that actually happened. Even the Roman laws laid down a penalty for just such a crime. And Oesterley tells us that in India one of the direst threats that one man can make to another is, 'I will sow bad wheat in your field.' In days of feuds and quarrels and lawlessness, one of the most effective assaults was to make a raid on a man's ground and infect it with some harmful weed. An eastern story tells how a man repaid a grudge he had against his neighbour.

Finding one day in a valley a mass of Kusseb [a kind of reed] in seed, as tall as a man, he filled his mantle with the heads, went home and extracted the seeds. 'I went,' he said, 'to Abu Jassin's kitchen garden. It was freshly ploughed; there I scattered the Kusseb seeds. The new year had scarcely come before the garden was thick with Kusseb. From that day to this—it is now some ten years—he could not plough a single furrow in it for the mass of Kusseb, and his olive trees withered away.'

So in this parable, as so often, Jesus is taking a story from real life with a background that his listeners would all recognise.

A Lesson to Jesus' Disciples

As we have seen, very often parables have a traditional and a modern interpretation. It is so with this parable, and again we begin with the traditional.

In this parable Jesus was saying something which first of all his disciples needed to learn. The disciples were worried about the kind of people Jesus was gathering around him. They could see very well that a great many people whom the world counted very unsatisfactory crowded about Jesus; and even apart from those whom society branded as sinners, there were many, loosely attached to Jesus, whose lives would not bear close scrutiny. They could hardly help taking up this point of view. Part of the dream of the Jewish nation was that when the Messiah came there would emerge, not only world conquest for Israel, but a new and stainless humanity. They looked not only for political power but also for moral reformation when the Messiah came. In addition, many of the disciples had been attached to John the Baptist before Jesus arrived on the scene, and John's message had been distinctively ethical. He looked for one who was to come and purge the threshing floor and gather the wheat into the garner and cast the chaff into unquenchable fire.

Against all this background of thought the disciples were offended at the motley multitude who thronged around Jesus and they made it quite clear that they expected him to do some weeding out. There was always a certain intolerance in the minds of the disciples. When they saw someone casting out demons in the name of Jesus they told him to stop it because he was not one of them (Luke 9:49, 50). When a Gentile woman came seeking Jesus' help they fastidiously asked him to send her away because she was making a nuisance of herself (Matthew 15:23). When Jesus proposed to become a guest at the house of Zacchaeus they *all murmured*, and that undoubtedly includes the disciples (Luke 19:7). The disciples certainly were waiting for Jesus to sort out the mixed crowd who followed him.

A Lesson to the Pharisees

If that was so of the disciples, it was more so of the Scribes and Pharisees. It was one of their stock complaints that Jesus associated with tax-gathers and sinners (Matthew 9:11). They themselves would never have talked to, never have done business with, never have eaten with, never even have let the skirt of their robe touch a man who did not keep the law. They had divided the world into the good, who were themselves, and the bad who were all other people. One Rabbi's prayer went like this:

'I thank Thee that Thou hast put my part with those that sit in the Temple and not with those that sit at the street corner. I rise early and they rise early. I rise early to the words of the law; they rise early to vain things. I labour and they labour. I labour and receive a reward; they labour and receive no reward. I run and they run. I run to the life of the world to come; they run to destruction.'

The wide welcome of Jesus was flatly unintelligible to men with an outlook like that. If the disciples were *disappointed* that Jesus had not weeded out his followers, the Pharisees were *scandalised* that he had not done so.

So, in the face of that intolerance and that critical spirit which existed in the hearts of both of his own circle and of the Pharisees, Jesus
told this parable. On this interpretation, one of the main points is the
close resemblance between the darnel and the true wheat. The parable is a kind of extended commentary on the commandment, 'Judge
not that you be not judged' (Matthew 7:1). It tells men that they are
simply not able to distinguish between the good and the bad. If they
try to, the result will most probably be that they will destroy good and
bad alike. It teaches that judgment must be left to the end of the day
and committed to the hand of God.

There is indeed grave danger in judging other people. It is the
easiest thing in the world to judge completely wrongly. Collie Knox
tells of an incident from World War I. Knox and a friend were in
civilian clothes, lunching in a London restaurant. A young lady
came up and handed each of them a white feather. It was an intima-
tion that they were cowards because they were not obviously in the
armed forces. What she did not know was that Knox was recovering
from a crippling crash sustained while flying with the Royal Air
Force and that his friend had just come from Buckingham Palace
where he had been decorated for gallantry by the King. That girl had
exercised a judgment and how completely mistaken that judgment
was. It is the simple fact that it is not given to anyone to know all the
facts about anyone else. As Robert Burns said:

What's done we partly may compute,
But know not what's resisted.

Over and over again, to know all would indeed be to forgive all.

It is possible to condemn the finest actions simply because we
misunderstand them. Gladstone, the great Prime Minister, gave his
time generously to reforming fallen women in London. There were
those who ascribed his interest in these women to far less worthy
motives and who frankly spread the most malicious and evil-minded
gossip about him. The news reached the ears of Queen Victoria and

she treated him very coldly. There again we have the supreme danger of passing judgments on other people; and it is against these hasty judgments that the parable warns.

We may come at this another way. Remember again the close similarity between the wheat and the darnel. Let us ask the simple question: *When we think about it, of how many people would we be prepared to say, 'This person deserves to go to heaven; and this person is fit only to go to hell'?* Or as someone has put it, 'How many of us would dare to say without misgiving, "I am of the wheat"? How many would care to say, "I am of the tares"?'

The result is that we cannot do other than leave the judgments to God. Dr Samuel Johnson said, 'God himself does not propose to judge a man till he is dead. So why should I?' To God only are known all the facts, and God only can be the judge.

The Judgment of God

This leads us to the other side of the parable. It counsels patience on our part and bids us leave the judgement to God; but it includes the absolute certainty that some day selection will come. The darnel and the wheat might be allowed to grow together for many days, but in the end there comes a harvest and a time of separation. So the parable says to us, 'Be patient in your judgments; but remember that some day God's judgment inevitably will come.'

An Enemy has done this

Before we leave the older interpretation of the parable, there is one other point we must note. When the owner of the field is told of the darnel in his field his answer is, 'An enemy must have done this.' Here we are brought face to face with the fact that there is in this world a power hostile to God. We may call that power Satan, the Devil, the tempter, but it is there.

Robert Louis Stevenson said, 'You know that Caledonian Railway Station in Princes Street, Edinburgh? One day I met Satan there.' No one knows what experience Stevenson had, but everyone who has any experience of life knows what he means. There are times when an evil power seems to assault us and seeks to draw us away from God. The old Persian religion believed that the whole universe was a battleground between the god of light and the god of darkness. And it believed that a man must take his stand on one side or the other, because he could not stand neutral. Inevitably the attack of the dark would come upon him and the appeal of the light would challenge him.

The why and wherefore of this are not the point. Jesus spent little time vainly speculating where evil came from; but he recognised, because he had experience of it, that evil power which assaults men and women; and he told them that the way to safety is never to walk alone but always to walk with him.

The Kingdom has come

The more modern interpretation of the parable is based entirely on the last verse (v 30). This interpretation holds that the disciples in effect said to Jesus, 'You say that the Kingdom has come. How can the Kingdom possibly have come when there are still so many bad people in the world?' To that question the parable is the answer, the gist of it being, 'No farmer would delay his harvesting just because there are some weeds about. He knows there are weeds; there never was a harvest without weeds; and therefore, weeds or no weeds, when the harvest is come he reaps.' So then, sinners or no sinners, the Kingdom is here and God's reaping is begun.

There is truth here. Remember again that Jesus, because of his utter acceptance of God's will, was the very embodiment of the Kingdom; and just because of that, a person's reaction to Jesus demonstrated unquestionably what kind of a person he or she was. Therefore by his acceptance or rejection of Jesus, an individual has automatically placed himself among the wheat or the tares. It is not so much that God has judged him; he has judged himself. In that sense indeed the harvest is come.

6

Of Every Kind

Matthew 13:47,48

The Seine Net

WE take this parable next because there are close connections between its thought and the thought of the parable of the Wheat and the Tares. This parable is usually called the Parable of the Drag-net. The *drag-net* is what we know as the *seine net*, a large net which has corks at the top and weights at the bottom, so that it stands, as it were, upright in the sea. Ropes attached to its four corners draw it through the sea, and as it is drawn it forms a cone-shaped cavity into which all kinds of sea creatures and various things are swept. In Galilee the net was then drawn to the shore and the fishermen sat down and sorted out its contents. The fish which could be used were put into vessels. (Perhaps these vessels were water tanks where the fish could be kept alive so that they could be delivered absolutely fresh to the market.) But the useless and unusable things were cast away.

The Picture of the Church

This parable gives us a vivid and valuable picture of the Kingdom; and it throws a shining light on the Church which is the instrument of the Kingdom upon earth.

Of Every Kind

Strong stress is put on the fact that the seine net gathers into its cone every kind of creature and thing. Surely this paints a clear picture of the all-embracing invitation of Christ and his Church. As someone has said, it lays down that there must be no selectiveness in the preaching of the gospel. To us that is something of a common-place. Throughout the years and the centuries we have come to think automatically that the gospel is for everyone. But to the ancient world this was an amazing thing. The ancient world everywhere was a world of barriers and of contempts.

In the *Greek* world there were three great divisions.

(1) There was the division between the Greek and the barbarian. The Greek was the man who spoke Greek, that beautiful, flexible, meaningful language of which men were well proud; and then there was the other man, the man who said 'bar bar', who uttered uncouth sounds in a strange tongue. The Greek began by looking with contempt on this man who knew no Greek.

(2) There was the division between the slave and the free man. In ancient Greece that was much more than a mere economic and social distinction. It was a fundamental difference. Aristotle had laid it down that there were certain men and women born to be hewers of wood and drawers of water. To improve their status was wrong because they existed solely to relieve the cultured classes from the routine tasks of life and work. So the free-born Greek looked with contempt upon the slave.

(3) There was the division between the wise and the ignorant. Plato had written above the door of the Academy, 'Let no one ignorant of geometry enter here.' There were the philosophers who spent their lives seeking to become wise in the things of gods and men, and there were the others, the simple folk with simple minds; and the wise man looked with contempt on the ignorant and the simple.

The *Roman* world, broadly speaking, divided men into Roman citizens and the rest. There were Romans and there were the lesser breeds. It is true that there was a time when Rome was truly great and when she saw her destiny in the task of imposing just and equitable law on the world, of bringing the Roman peace to all the world, of casting down the arrogant and sparing the conquered. But in the later days, when she had degenerated, Rome very largely saw the world as a place to be exploited for the ease and comfort of the Roman citizen.

The *Jewish* world had more barriers than any other.

(1) There was the barrier between Jew and Gentile. At their most extreme and arrogant the Jews believed that they were the only nation in the world for which God cared. They could and did say the

most terrible things. 'The best of the Gentiles kill; the best of the serpents crush.' 'The Lord is only gracious to the Israelites; other nations he will crush.' 'The heathen are not to be pushed into a pit to die, but if they should fall in there is no reason why they should be helped out.' The Jew looked with contempt on the man of any other race.

(2) There was the barrier between man and woman. Officially women were despised. That is not to say that there were not the truest of family relationships among the Jews. There will never be a land or a race where the mother of the family does not matter. But, in his morning prayer, the Jew thanked God that, 'Thou hast not created me a Gentile, a slave or a woman.' It was considered that to educate a woman was equivalent to casting pearls before swine. The strict Rabbi would not be seen talking to a woman in public, not even to his own wife or sister. The official attitude was that women did not matter.

(3) There was the barrier between the man who kept the Law and the man who did not. The Pharisees kept every smallest detail of the ceremonial law. They had a technical term for the people who did not—they called them 'The People of the Land.' It was nothing less than a crime for one who kept the law to marry, or to allow any of his family, to marry one of the common people of the land. They would do no business with them; they would neither give them any hospitality nor receive any hospitality from them. They would not even share a journey with them. They had a saying: 'He who gives bread to a man who observes not the Law will suffer for it.' They had an utter contempt for the man who did not keep the Law.

(4) There was the barrier between good and bad. It is true that goodness and badness were largely interpreted in terms of keeping or not keeping the ceremonial Law. But it went beyond that. They were prepared to say, 'There is joy in heaven over one sinner who is wiped out.' Nowhere is this better seen than in the story of the woman taken in adultery (John 8:1-11). According to the Jewish law those who wished to stone the woman to death were quite correct. Unquestionably the penalty laid down for one taken in the act of adultery was that he or she should be stoned to death. But what no one can fail to see in that story is that those who wished to stone the

woman did not regard the stoning as a bit of harsh justice which with sorrow they were bound to inflict; it was something in which they were going to find grim and sadistic joy.

That was typical of the attitude of those who regarded themselves as good to those whom they considered bad. That is why the Jewish leaders were shocked to the core when Jesus showed himself the friend of sinners and outcasts. It is worthy of consideration that frequently we begin a service with the verses of Psalm 24, 'Who shall ascend the hill of the Lord, and who shall stand in his holy place? He who has clean hands and a pure heart; who does not lift up his soul to what is false, and does not swear deceitfully. He will receive blessing from the Lord and vindication from the God of his salvation' (vv 3-5). What we often fail to realise is that this approach is far more a Jewish than a Christian one, and that in fact it shuts every one of us out from the presence of God without the merits and the grace of Christ. So then the Jew had an utter contempt for the sinner.

The Modern Barriers

This parable stresses the all-inclusive, non-selective invitation of Christ. We have seen how new that wide invitation was to the ancient world, but it is still to be stressed, for there still exists the sin of exclusiveness and of contempt.

(1) There is sometime contempt for those we regard as sunk so low as to be irreclaimable. In the Middle Ages there was a great scholar called Muretus. He was, as most scholars were, very poor. He wandered from place to place teaching and learning. He fell seriously ill in a certain Italian city. No one knew who he was and he was regarded as simply a vagrant without resources. The doctors were discussing his case and they were suggesting that, since he was obviously of no use to anyone, it did not much matter what happened to him anyway. They were speaking in Latin, the scholar's language, never dreaming that he understood; and when they had finished he looked up and said, 'Call no man worthless for whom Christ died.'

(2) There is the obvious instance of colour prejudice. Even when we are trying to overcome this prejudice, too often our attitude to

people of other colours is that of a consciously gracious condescension and not that of those who treat everyone equally.

(3) There is still the attitude of those who think they are good to those they think are bad. In London's dock district there was a woman who lived with a Chinese man. She found her way somehow or other to a Women's Meeting in a church and brought her child who was half Chinese. She liked it and came back. But at her second visit the minister of the church asked her not to come back again. He explained that the other women had said that if she came they could not possibly come because they could not associate with people like her. She answered wistfully, 'Sir, I know I'm a sinner; but isn't there anywhere a sinner can go?'

If at any time we feel this attitude of contempt, or realise that we are drifting into exclusiveness, we must remember the parable which tells that the Kingdom is like a net which gathers every kind.

The Mixture of the Church

We may come at this another way, for it will enable us to understand a very real problem and to answer a very common accusation. There is inherent in this parable the implication that the Church will always be a mixture. It has always been one of the accusations levelled against the Church that it has so many unsatisfactory members; that, in fact, the people inside it are little or no better than the people outside it. The plain implication of this parable is that it cannot be any other way, because the net as it sweeps the sea gathers all kinds of things into itself.

We can go further than that. The very same accusation, in principle, was levelled against Jesus. He was accused of being surrounded by extremely unsatisfactory people. His answer still stands: 'Those who are well have no need of a physician, but those who are sick' (Matthew 9:12). Someone has said that you could not possibly use it as an accusation against a hospital that it is full of people who are ill. It is precisely to take these people that it exists. Its job, the reason for its being, is to cure such people. There is indeed something wrong with a Church which has no effect on the lives of its people;

but a Church which welcomes sinners is only fulfilling its true function.

We must remember two things. First, if the Church were a place for perfect people there would be no members at all. Second, as has been said long ago, what really matters is not so much where a man is, as the direction in which he is facing. The Church must remain a mixture, but if she is acting as the physician of Christ, and if the people in her are facing in the right direction, facing Christ, then the fact that she is a mixture is her glory and not her condemnation.

There is Selection

But there is another side. The parable lays down unmistakably that there is a process of selection going on. They did gather the good into vessels and they did throw the bad away.

Scholars are fairly well agreed that the original parable stops at verse 48 and that verses 49 and 50 are later additions. If we stop at verse 48 we see that this process of selection is happening *here and now*. It is on the moment that the selection between the good and bad is being made. That is true of all life. Every moment we are judging ourselves. That is why what we call trivialities are so important; in every tiny action we show whether we are courteous, whether we are kind, whether we are considerate and sympathetic, whether we are scrupulously honest, whether we set the highest value on the right things.

In the word *crisis* we have taken over a Greek word literally. In Greek *krisis* means a judgment: in English *crisis* means a great occasion. The way in which a man meets a *crisis* is a *krisis*; in that moment he judges himself. So we are back to the point we have made so repeatedly. When a man is faced with Jesus Christ, that is *the supreme crisis*; his reaction is his judgment on himself, *the supreme krisis*. Therefore judgment is not delayed until eternity, for we are judging ourselves in every action every day. We are deciding whether we are the good who are gathered in, or the bad who are cast away.

7

When it is Grown

Matthew 13:31,32; Mark 4:30-32; Luke 13:18,19

The Smallest of All

THERE is a very important difference in the point of this Parable of the Mustard Seed as it is narrated in Matthew and Mark and as it is narrated in Luke. Let us begin with the version of Matthew and Mark.

In Palestine the mustard seed was proverbial for the smallest of all things. It is not strictly true that it is the smallest of all seeds; the cypress seed, for instance, is still smaller. But it was universally used as the type of anything that was infinitesimally small. The Rabbis spoke of 'a spot or blemish as small as a mustard seed.' In Matthew 17:20 Jesus spoke of faith as a mustard seed. To this day the Arabs have a phrase about faith weighing not more than a grain of mustard seed.

The Smallest becomes the Greatest

In Matthew and in Mark the clear point of the parable is the fact that in time the smallest seed grows into the largest of herbs. Mustard in Palestine was not a garden plant at all but a field plant, because of the height to which it grew. It commonly grew to a height of seven or eight feet and its branches did look like the branches of a tree. A traveller in Palestine says, 'With the help of my guide I uprooted a veritable mustard tree which was more than twelve feet high. In the presence of such stout branches which overtop all surrounding herbs there is no exaggeration in the parable of the mustard seed.' It is quite true that birds come and nest in its branches. They are often to be seen settled in flocks on the mustard plants because they love the little black seeds which they pick out of the pods. So then the first lesson of the parable is that though a thing may start from the smallest beginnings, it may end by being something very great.

The Parable and the Disciples

When it was first spoken this parable had a special message for the disciples themselves. There is no doubt that they were bewildered and discouraged. They had hoped for so much and so little had happened. It seemed in fact that even the little that had happened was in serious danger of being engulfed by the growing waves of opposition to Jesus. The mission of John the Baptist had been extremely impressive; the crowds had flocked out to listen to him and to accept his baptism. And John himself had clearly stated that still greater days were to come and still greater things were to happen. He told them that among them there was one whose shoe he was not worthy to untie, and whose baptism was far beyond anything that he could offer or do (Matthew 3:11; Mark 1:7; Luke 3:16; John 1:26,27). John told them that he must inevitably decrease, but this great one who was to come after him must inevitably increase (John 3:30).

Words like that could not do anything but prepare the minds of the disciples for impressive and sensational happenings. At first when the crowds flocked after Jesus it must have looked as if this were coming true; but bit by bit the opposition increased. The crowds abandoned him; and it was already clear that the mission of Jesus which had started with such promise was likely to issue in failure and disaster. They had begun with such high hopes and these hopes were now apparently to be disappointed. So Jesus told this parable to help them see that the beginnings might seem small, but no man knew to what they would yet grow. And surely it is impossible for them to have listened to that parable and to have glimpsed its meaning without the dawning conviction that *they* were the small beginning and that everything depended on them.

The Universal Truth

Apart from that truth which the parable sought to make plain to the disciples, it lays down a truth which is universal and valid for all time. Always the greatest things start from the smallest beginnings. All music comes from the octave. From these eight notes comes every hymn, every song, every concerto, every symphony, every oratorio that was ever written. In the last analysis all literature is built on the 26 letters of the alphabet. From them come every novel, every treatise, every poem, every speech which was ever made. We live in an age which worships size and numbers. Yet history proves again and again that it is not the big things but the small beginnings which are of paramount importance.

On 11 December 1620 a ship called 'The Mayflower' set sail from England to America because the people in her could not find the religious liberty they desired. On that ship there were only 101 people; and she herself was but a tiny thing. Yet the plain fact of history is that this voyage from Plymouth in 1620 by that little ship and that little group did more to change the world than any of the voyages of the great liners in the centuries to come.

A staggering thing to think about is the smallness of the number of people who can ever have seen or heard Jesus. In our world of radio and television, and of newspapers which number their circulation by the million, a person who has something notable to say may be sure that his or her message can become known overnight to the whole world. But, as Acts 1:15 tells us, the total number of the Christian Church after the life, death, resurrection and ascension of Jesus was 120. Yet out of that small beginning came the Christian Church as we know it today. We must never be discouraged by small beginnings and by the apparently infinitesimal effect that we can have. If a thing is right it has God behind it, and in the end it will make its mark.

Christianity, a Living Organism

Further, this parable teaches that Christianity is a living organism. All the time the mustard seed was growing. From day to day and from hour to hour that growth was not measurable; but when the beginning was compared with the end, the growth was plain for all to see. It is characteristic of our age that we want to see things happen in the flash of an eye. Very seldom do the great things happen that way.

There is an experiment which shows the effect of small forces on great masses. It can be performed in two ways. One is to suspend from the ceiling a block of iron weighing more than a hundredweight; and to suspend beside it a cork which weights less than an ounce. The cork is then swung against the iron in little blows. It seems impossible that the gentle taps of the cork will ever have any effect on the mass of iron and indeed at first nothing seems to happen. But after a while the iron begin to tremble, then to move; and finally it is swinging in a wide arc as a result of the continuous tapping of the cork. Lord Kelvin performed the same experiment in an even more vivid way. He supplied himself with little pellets of paper about the size of a pea; and began to pelt the iron mass with the pellets of paper. At first nothing happened, but after a time the iron began to vibrate; then to sway; until finally it was swinging freely. We may think that anything we do is so little as to be ineffective; but the cumulative effect of the small efforts of every man can be used mightily by God in the bringing in of his Kingdom.

The Conversion of the Soul

This parable has a very definite relevance to the question of conversion. One of the supreme faults in any sphere of human experience is to take one type of experience and insist that it alone is the pattern to which all other experience must conform. It is a great disaster, and sometimes a tragedy, that conversion has been so often associated with something which happens as suddenly as a lightning flash.

The experience of Paul on the Damascus Road has been taken mistakenly as a standard for all conversion experience. Consider what Paul was doing when he met Christ on the Damascus Road. He was filled with one dominating desire—to eliminate the very name of Jesus from the world. He was actually on the way to persecute Christians and, if possible, to wipe out the Church completely. What happened to Paul was indeed a sudden reversal which turned his life upside down. Many came into the Church in the early days direct from heathenism. They had already been worshipping strange gods; they already possessed a creed of belief and an ethical system. If they were to become Christians at all they had to make a radical change in their way of life. For such people conversion was necessarily sudden; they were coming from ignorance to knowledge, and not infrequently from hostility to submission.

That may still be the case. But think of a young person brought up in a Christian home. As soon as he heard anything he heard the name of Jesus. As soon as he could speak he was taught to pray. It may well be that from the age of three or four he was at Sunday School and within the fellowship of the Church. Never at any time did he seek to destroy the name of Christ or to wipe out the Christian Church. Never at any time did he worship pagan gods and follow a life of immorality. Once Thoreau was asked, 'Have you made your peace with God?' 'I never knew,' he said, 'that he was my enemy.'

There is a radical difference here. In the early days and sometimes even still, a man is coming from hostility to Christ to love for Christ. But in the case of the child born into a Christian home, he (or she) grows deeper and deeper into Christianity; he learns more and more about Christ; as the years go on the Jesus who was ever dear becomes dearer yet, until by the most natural process in the world he comes, certainly with decision, but with no shattering shock, to accept Jesus Christ as his Saviour, his Master and his Lord.

There are two ways to open a door and see into a room. With one violent wrench we may open the door so that the room lies disclosed to sight. Or we may open the door gradually until little by little the whole room lies revealed. Let no man think he has missed something because he has not had the shattering experience Paul had on the way to Damascus. The person who has always known Christ grows a little more every day as a flower in the sun.

The Tree and the Branches

Now we must turn to Luke's version of this parable. Luke makes no mention at all of the smallness of the seed. His point is that some day the birds of the air came and lodged in the branches. In eastern thought one of the most common pictures of a great empire was to visualise it as a great tree with many branches; and the birds on the branches are the subject peoples who are part of that great empire and who find their peace and safety within it. Ezekiel makes use of this picture in 17:22-24 and 31:3ff. So then Luke's idea is that the parable means that the Kingdom is like a great tree with many branches in which many peoples shall find rest.

The Branches of the Church

Here is a great thought. By implication it means that it does not matter how many branches there are in the Church so long as they are all stemmed in Christ. Here is a warning against exclusiveness. So often people insist that their way is the only way, and that their Church alone has the way to salvation:

> *We are God's chosen few;*
> *All others will be damned;*
> *There is no room in heaven for you—*
> *We can't have heaven crammed.*

John Wesley was the very opposite of that. When his nephew entered the Roman Catholic Church, Wesley was deeply grieved. But he did not upbraid him; he wished him well. He said, 'You can be saved in any Church and you can be damned in any Church. What matters is, How is your heart with Christ?' Wesley's greeting to all men was, 'Is your heart as my heart? Then give me your hand.' The Methodist invitation to the Lord's Table is 'for all those who love the Lord.' It does not matter whether or not there are many branches of the Church. What matters is that they should all remember they are stemmed in Christ and that they should remember the Master who unites them, not the differences which divide them.

Fellowship in Difference

Sometimes the fact that there are so many branches of the Church is used as a condemnation. In point of fact it is the Church's great virtue and blessing. Not all people worship alike. Some find God in a bare simplicity; others in an elaborate form of worship. Some find him in speech, some in music, some in silence. Amidst the multiplicity of

45

Churches an individual can find that Church in which he or she will find God.

Nothing could be less desirable than one great mechanically united Church in which there was a flat similarity in ritual and in worship. Its very diversity is the glory of the Protestant Church. But just because of that it is of intense importance that every branch of the Church should remember that it is stemmed in Christ. There is nothing wrong in a man thinking of himself as a member of a congregation and being proud of it; in thinking of himself as a member of a certain branch of the Church and loving its traditions; but beyond his congregation and beyond his branch of the Church, he must remember that he is a member of the Church of Christ.

We may take a parallel from the Army. A veteran of World War II may have been in the Argyll and Sutherland Highlanders and he is right to be proud of the tradition of the Argylls. But the Argylls were part of the Fifty-first Division and it too had a record for pride. The Fifty-first Division was part of the Eighth Army and the Eighth Army had a unique record. The Eighth Army was part of His Majesty's Forces. So in the Church, by all means let us take pride in our own branch; and by all means let us set our faces against a flat uniformity; but amidst the differences let us remember the Christ who unites us, the tree in whom all the branches are stemmed and from whom all draw their life.

8

Till the Whole was Leavened
Matthew 13:33; Luke 13:20,21

A Story from Home

IN this case, when Jesus wanted a picture of the Kingdom, he went back home for it. In Palestine, at least in the smaller towns and villages, there was no such thing as a baker's shop; bread was made at home. Often Jesus had seen his mother Mary baking. When she was baking bread she took *leaven*, dough which had been kept over from a previous baking and which, in the keeping, had fermented. The leaven inserted in the dough changed the whole character of the bread which emerged. So Jesus says, 'Just at the leaven changes the character of the dough into which it is inserted, so the Kingdom changes all things.'

Leaven

There is one difficulty in this parable. Very commonly, leaven in Hebrew thought and language was a synonym for evil influence. It is always so elsewhere in the New Testament. In Mark 8:15 Jesus advised his disciples to beware of the leaven of the Pharisees and of Herod. Twice (1 Corinthians 5:6, Galatians 5:9) Paul uses the phrase, 'A little leaven leavens the whole lump'; when he is exhorting people to have nothing to do with things which can be evil influences. When a man entered the Jewish religion and then relapsed into Gentile ways, he was said by the Rabbis 'to return to his leaven.' The Jews believed that in man there were two opposite tendencies, one drawing him to goodness and the other to evil. They called these tendencies the good nature and the bad nature; and sometimes they called the bad nature the *leaven*. At the coming of the Passover Feast every scrap of leaven had to be cleared out of the house.

It is certainly true that the Jews usually used leaven as a synonym for bad influence. That was probably because they identified fermentation with rottenness and leaven seemed to them something which introduced decay into that into which it was placed. But at the same time leaven is sometimes used in a good sense. One Rabbi said, 'Great is peace in that peace is to the earth as is the leaven to the dough.' Although usually used in a bad sense, leaven could be used for any invasive and pervasive influence.

The Disturbing Element

There are differing interpretations of this parable, although they come to much the same meaning in the end. C H Dodd, for example, saw it as a symbol of the disturbing influence of Christianity. 'We should observe,' he said, 'that the working of the leaven in the dough is not a slow imperceptible process. At first it is true the leaven is hidden and nothing appears to happen; but soon the whole mass swells and bubbles as fermentation rapidly advances.' As the leaven turned the dough into a seething mass, so the influence of Christianity was profoundly disturbing.

Now it is true that real religion is always a disturbing thing. When Ahab the evil king came face to face with Elijah the disturbing prophet, he said to him, 'Is it you, you troubler of Israel?' (1 Kings 18:17). In one sense it was the duty of the prophet to trouble his fellow countrymen and make them think. When Christianity first came to Thessalonica the cry was, 'These men who have turned the world upside down have come here also' (Acts 17:6). In Philippi the accusation against Paul and his friends was, 'These men are Jews and they are disturbing our city' (Acts 16:20). Real religion is always disturbing.

The Christian Revolution

We do well to remember this. It has been sometimes levelled as a charge against Christianity that it was dope, 'the opiate of the people', and that it taught men to endure things against which they should have rebelled. True Christianity, on the contrary, is always revolutionary.

Stanley Jones has been pointed out that the Magnificat (Luke 1:46-55) is one of the most revolutionary documents in the world. Let us take some verses of it:

He has shown strength with his arm,
he has scattered the proud in the imagination of their hearts,
he has put down the mighty from their thrones,
and exalted those of low degree;
he has filled the hungry with good things,
and the rich he has sent empty away.

(Luke 1:51-53)

In these three verses are three revolutions which true Christianity is bound to carry out.

(1) There is a *moral* revolution. The proud are brought down. Christianity must begin by working a revolution within a man's own heart. It does that by making him see what he really is. Alcibiades, a wild and reckless young man, was a close friend, strangely enough, of Socrates. But sometimes he used to say to Socrates, 'Socrates, I hate you; for every time I meet you, you make me realise what I am.' When a man meets Jesus Christ he cannot but compare his life with Jesus' life and the comparison can bring nothing but shame. We may think we play golf or tennis well; but if we go to see one of the masters we know just how inadequate we are. So when we set our lives beside the life of the Lord of all good life, we know how far we fall short. Further, when a man realises the love of God in Christ and the lengths to which that love went, he cannot but be amazed that this was done for him. And he must then be filled with the desire to change himself until somehow he becomes worthy of a sacrifice like that.

(2) There is a *social* revolution. The mighty are brought low and those of low degree are exalted. This is because Christianity has no respect for the labels which the world attaches to a person. The world places a man according to the size of his bank account, the number of people he controls, his prestige in whatever field his work may happen to lie. Christianity rates a man by the service that he renders to his fellow men. 'Whoever would be first among you

must be slave of all' (Mark 10:44). The result is that the man whom the world accounts great may well be worthless in the Kingdom of God; while the man who appears of no standing in the world may well be greatest. In the old days in Russia there was a nobleman who kept open house. Anyone who wished might come and sit at his table. A man's place at that table was decided by one simple test. When he arrived the nobleman would say, 'Show me your hands.' If the hands were toil worn, the guest received a high place; but if they were soft and flabby, he was directed to the lowest seat. So the test in the Kingdom is the test of service.

(3) There is an *economic* revolution. The hungry are filled with good things and the rich are sent empty away. In the truly Christian state there would be such a feeling of responsibility that no one could bear to have too much while others had too little. Branscomb, an American theologian, put it this way:

> Business would be run not for its owners only but to support the needs of the community; no farmer would plough solely for financial gain but to feed a hungry world; no doctor or lawyer would practise for himself alone but to heal and help those in distress. Every work would be directed to the healing, the helping and the supplying of the spiritual and the physical needs of men. This would lend every task its glory; he would be greatest who was the greatest servant of all.

An economic revolution is the Christian aim.

It is then clear that if you take the leaven as a disturbing influence in the dough, this parable teaches the disturbing influence of Christianity on the life of the individual and the life of the world.

The Imperceptible Influence

But there are more ways than one of interpreting this parable. It is possible to argue that the leaven stands for the imperceptible influence of the Kingdom. We can no more see the leaven working than we can see a flower growing, but working it is all the time. And so is the power of the Kingdom. One of the most common debates is, 'Is the world getting better or worse?' Oliver Cromwell said of his son Richard's education, 'I would have him know a little history.' To the person who knows anything of history there is only one answer to that question—the world is getting better.

When we look at things, not so much year to year as age to age, we see the difference. Here is a quotation from Seneca, the great Stoic philosopher, who lived at the same time as Paul. (Some people think that he may even have known Paul.) He writes, 'We strangle a mad dog; we slaughter a fierce ox; we plunge the knife into sickly cattle lest they taint the herd; *children who are born deformed or weakly we drown.*' In the sands of the Egyptian desert it is still possible to dig up letters written on papyrus. Some of them are private letters such as anyone might write to his friend or relation. Here is one, dated AD 1.

Hilarion to Alis his wife heartiest greetings, and to my dear Berous and to Apollonarion. I want you to know that we are still in Alexandria. Don't worry if when all the others come back I stay on in Alexandria. I beg and beseech you to look after the little child and as soon as we get our wages I'll send something up to you. If—good luck be with you—you bear a child, if it is a boy, let it live; if it is a girl, throw it out. You told Aphrodisias to say to me not to forget you. How can I forget you? So I beg you not to worry.

It is a strange letter with its mixture of deep affection and absolute mercilessness. Now we could not possibly imagine anyone in a civilised country today talking about slaughtering weakly children or throwing out baby girls. Yet that was the normal custom when Christianity came into the world. Why the change? It is not that the world is yet a Christian world; but the influence of Christian ideals has so permeated society that certain things can no longer be entertained. Imperceptibly but surely, the influence of the Kingdom is there.

Further, this parable teaches that the influence which changes mankind must come from the inside. Before any result could follow, the leaven had to be inserted inside the dough. We live in an age which sets great store on external changes. We believe that, if we can give people better houses and working conditions, we will make better people. It is true that the influence of the Church must be with all efforts to improve the lot of men, but the fact remains that no man is changed until his heart is changed.

Nathaniel Hawthorne has a parable entitled 'The Holocaust.' In it he pictures a bonfire of all the evil things in the world. The devil is looking on and is naturally discouraged and worried. But in the end he brightens up. 'I am not done yet,' he says. 'They have forgotten one thing—they have forgotten to throw in a human heart.' It is not the primary function of Christianity to make new conditions, but to make new men and women. If that is done then new conditions will inevitably follow; but to start with the conditions is to put the cart before the horse.

The Power from Outside

There is another truth which follows naturally from that which we have been considering. The dough had no power to change itself. The power which was to change it—the leaven—had to come from outside. Just so, men and women have no power to change themselves. We know that from experience. There can be few people who have not made their resolutions and their plans and seen these same resolution and plans come to nothing.

Archimedes discovered that if you placed a lever below a mass you could lift the mass, and the longer the lever the bigger the mass that could be lifted. In the end he came to this conclusion. 'Give me a lever long enough,' he said, 'and give me a place outside the world to stand and I will lift the world.' He knew well that the lifting must come from outside. If we are to be changed, and if the world is to be changed, that change must come from a power that is not our power, *ie* the power of Christ. 'If anyone is in Christ he is a new creation; the old has passed away, behold, the new has come' (2 Corinthians 5:17). The risen Christ said, 'Behold I make all things new' (Revelation 21:5).

The Lesson to the Jews

There is one other lesson in this parable which may have been meant specifically for the Jews. When the leaven was put into the dough it was dispersed. It ceased to exist by itself, but by losing its own existence it altered the whole character of the dough. It may be that Jesus was foreseeing things. Perhaps he saw a day when the Jewish nation would be destroyed and scattered and the Temple desolate. And yet that very dispersal of the Jews was to change the world. The Jews would lose their nationhood and yet would do something for the world which no one else could do.

Such influence indeed did they have on the world that the Romans used to say that the conquered had given laws to the conquerors. When the Jews were scattered they took with them their synagogues, so that there was a synagogue in almost every town of importance in the world; their Law and their scriptures, so that many non-Jews knew the Old Testament; their God, so that many a heathen knew something of the true God; their Sabbath, so that men knew of a day when earthly things were laid by and they thought of God. The dispersal of the Jews was in a real sense the leaven which prepared the world for the spread of Christianity.

9

Hid in a Field

Matthew 13:44 .

The Hidden Treasure

TO modern western ears this may sound a most unlikely story, but as usual Jesus was in fact telling of something that frequently happened in Palestine.

Palestine was a land of wars. At any time a man's back garden might become a battleground and his house looted; and so to hide one's valuables in the ground was one of the most common ways of preserving one's property. The Rabbis indeed had a proverbial saying, 'There is only one safe repository for money—the earth.'

Folk-lore was full of just such tales as this. There is one about Alexander the Great. He was once present when the king of a certain country was called upon to decide a case. A man who had found a treasure in a field which he had bought from another, wished to return it to the seller, who refused to take it on the grounds that he had sold the field with all its contents. The king settled the matter by deciding that the treasure should be given as a dowry to the daughter of the one man: she was going to marry the son of the other. Alexander laughed and said that in his country the king would certainly have killed both men and confiscated the money.

Apollonius of Tyana tells another. He was consulted by an Indian king about a puzzling case. A man had found a chest of treasure in a piece of land that he had bought and the former owner was claiming it. Apollonius gave it as his verdict that an inquiry should be held into the character of both men, for, he said, he could not believe that the gods would deprive the one of his land unless he were a bad man; or that they would give to the other what was below the ground unless he were a better man. Investigation was made and sure enough the seller was a rascal who had neglected to sacrifice to the gods; and the finder was devout and pious.

The story Jesus told was not of an improbable happening. It was about something which happened so often that many such stories circulated.

The Legal Position

To some minds this parable presents something of a moral problem. When the man found the treasure, he immediately concealed it and rushed off to buy the field without revealing what was in it. Doesn't this sound very like sharp practice? There are three possible ways in which that objection may be met.

(1) It may be that the man was well within his rights. The Jewish Talmud law regarding findings was quite clear. 'What belongs to the finder and about what must information be given? These things belong to the finder—if a man finds scattered fruit or scattered money, these belong to the finder.' It would then seem that the man was within his rights. And yet the whole parable has an atmosphere of haste. Why the haste to purchase the field if the treasure legally belonged to the finder anyway?

(2) It has been suggested that Jesus is deliberately telling the story of a sharp-dealing rascal; and that he is in effect saying, 'If a man will go to all that trouble to get a treasure that perishes, how much more should you bend all your energies and make every sacrifice to get the treasure that matters most of all?' In other words, 'If only Christians were as much in earnest about the things of the Kingdom as sharp-witted business men are about the things of business, what a difference it would make.'

(3) C H Dodds, however, holds that all such discussion is irrelevant: to treat the parable in this way is to make it an allegory, which is just what we must not do. The one point of the parable is the finding of the treasure and the sacrificing of everything for it; just so, a man should sacrifice everything for the Kingdom of God.

The Accidental Discovery

When we come to the meaning of the parable, the first thing that stands out is the accidental way in which the treasure was discovered. It was found when the man was never looking for it. There have also been people who met Jesus Christ in what looks like a completely accidental way. Let us take two examples.

(1) The first concerns C H Spurgeon, to whom many owed their souls. As a boy of 15, he set off one New Year's morning for church, but there was such a blizzard of snow that he was not able to reach the church he was in the habit of attending. 'When I could go no farther,' he said, 'I turned down a court and came to a little Primitive Methodist Chapel.' The preacher who was to have conducted the service never got there for he too was held up by the weather, and quickly one of the office-bearers has to be brought forward to conduct the service with a congregation of perhaps 15 people. 'The man,' said Spurgeon, 'was really stupid. His text was "Look unto me and by ye saved all the ends of the earth," and he kept repeating it because he had nothing else to say.' Something about young Spurgeon caught the impromptu preacher's eye. 'Young man,' he said suddenly, 'you look very miserable; and you will always be miserable—miserable in life and miserable in death—if you do not obey my text.' Then suddenly he literally shouted, 'Young man, look to Jesus! Look, look, look!' 'And,' said Spurgeon, 'I did and then and there the cloud was gone, the darkness had rolled away, and that moment I saw the sun!' It looked like a series of sheer accidents which made Spurgeon stumble on the grace of God.

(2) Another example is medical missionary Sir Wilfred Grenfell. As a student he had been visiting an out-patient in a London district. On the way home he turned out of curiosity into a big tent where, as it happened, a mission was being conducted by Moody and Sankey. 'It was so new to me,' he said, 'that when a tedious prayer-bore began with a long oration, I started to leave. Suddenly the leader, whom I learned afterwards was D L Moody, called out to the audience, "Let us sing a hymn while our brother finishes his prayer." His practicability interested me and I stayed the service out. When eventually I left, it was with a determination either to make religion a real effort to do as I thought Christ would do in my place as a doctor, or frankly abandon it.' The turning point in Grenfell's career was a chance visit

to an evangelical mission and a most unconventional remark by D L Moody.

It often happened that Jesus came most unexpectedly into a man's life. Surely the extreme example is Simon of Cyrene. It was the ambition of every Jew once in a lifetime to attend the Passover at Jerusalem. Jews who stayed abroad would scrape and pinch and save for half a lifetime to make that possible. Doubtless that is what Simon did; and then, when he was making his way to the holy city and the sacred Temple, he suddenly found himself with shattering unexpectedness carrying a cross (Matthew 27:32). Surely the explanation is that God is looking for us even before we look for him.

All in the Day's Work

Another thing emerges—it is implied that it was at his day's work that this man found the treasure. He was digging in the field when all of a sudden his spade hit against the treasure and his world was changed. And often it is in the day's work we are likely to come up against God.

It is one of the amazing facts of life that the day's work can produce the greatest things. Take the case of J S Bach. For years he was teacher and organist in St Thomas' School, Leipzig. For £125 a year he had to train the boys' choir, play at services, weddings and funerals, and—most amazing of all—produce new compositions every Sunday. They were never published; they were simply written, sung and then piled into a cupboard to grow old and dusty and forgotten. Priceless music—'Sheep may safely graze' and 'Jesu, joy of man's desiring', for example—was written, used and piled away. In 'the day's work' in Leipzig he produced 265 church cantatas; 263 chorales; 14 larger works; 24 secular cantatas; 6 concertos; 4 overtures; 18 piano and violin concertos; 356 organ works and 162 pieces for the piano.

As John Keble wrote:

The trivial round, the common task,
Will furnish all we ought to ask,

Room to deny ourselves, a road
To bring us daily nearer God.

It is not in longing for some other task than our own, but in doing our own faithfully and well, that we find happiness and God.

The Crucial Moment

There remains one other thing—the man in the parable seized the crucial moment when it came. When he found the treasure—and in his haste he cannot have stopped to examine it fully—he there and then sold everything and bought the field. It was so with Grenfell and with Spurgeon. They acted on the moment. James Russell Lowell, an American poet, wrote: *Once to every man and nation comes the moment to decide.*

Shakespeare, in Julius Caesar, said:

There is a tide in the affairs of men,
Which, taken at the flood, leads on to fortune;
Omitted, all the voyage of their life
Is bound in shallows and in miseries.

(IV: iii)

One of the gravest dangers in life is that we may be moved by some high impulse; but we do not act at once and the impulse dies. If we would possess the treasure of the Kingdom we must seize the great moments however unexpectedly they come—and they will come, not in times of laziness and of vain longings for what we have not got, but in *the day's work*.

10

He sold all that He had

Matthew 13:45,46

WHEN Jesus spoke this parable, pearls had a strange fascination for men. What we might call the worship of the pearl really came from Egypt, and from the Egyptians the Romans had learned it. The curious thing was that the pearl was not desired so much for its money value; simply to look at a pearl and handle it was a source of delight. In the Jewish Talmud the pearl is often spoken of as being beyond price. The pearl merchants scoured the world for really beautiful specimens. They found them in the Red Sea; but it was from the Persian Gulf, India and Britain, that the loveliest and the costliest pearls came.

The story of the parable is simple. It is about a man who had spent his life looking for the perfect pearl and when he found it he sold everything he had and bought it.

The Searcher

When we read first the story of the Hidden Treasure and then the story of the Pearl of Great Price, one thing immediately becomes clear. In one sense the one is the contrast and the complement of the other. It was apparently by the sheerest chance that the man found the hidden treasure; but it was at the end of a long search that the merchant man found the pearl he had been seeking all his life. So then, just as it is possible for a man to discover the Kingdom almost accidentally, it is also possible for him to arrive at it after a life-long search.

It was that way, for instance, with Paul. All his life Paul had been seeking the peace and the joy of God. It was that way with Martin Luther. Luther said that if ever a man could have been saved by monkery that man was he. It must have been that way with Nicodemus. He was a Rabbi and all his life he must have searched for God's truth. Justin

Martyr, one of the greatest of the second century fathers, tells us how he had wandered from philosophy to philosophy until finally he found the elusive secret of peace in Christianity.

There is a place in Christianity for the seeking mind. 'The unexamined life,' said Plato, 'is the life not worth living.' There is a duty on men to think things through. Even if a man finds the Kingdom suddenly he is not exempt from this duty; for he must still tease out the problem of what this means for him and for his life. No one should be ashamed of his questionings and doubts. So many people's faith collapses when it meets with trouble and sorrow and disaster simply because they have not thought things out.

Someone once said to an adventurous thinker, 'I skirted the howling deserts of infidelity.' The thinker replied, 'You would have done much better to struggle through them and come out on the other side.' It is always bad to suppress doubts. It is better to face them honestly, for it is better to have one or two things which we believe unquestionably than a whole host of things of whose truth we are entirely vague. No one can begin to test things during the storm. The test should be applied long before that.

The Necessary Sacrifice

The parable speaks also of the necessary sacrifice. To get the pearl of great price the merchant had to sell up all his possessions. To get the best he had to abandon the second best. And if we want the highest good there are certain subordinate goods that we may well have to give up.

(1) *We may have to give up material things.* A classic example is F W Charrington, who inherited the lucrative family brewing business. One day he was passing a pub when he saw a man, already under the influence, about to enter, while his wife tried to dissuade him. Suddenly the man turned and with one savage blow knocked the woman senseless. Charrington moved forward to help and, suddenly, he saw his own name above the pub door. With that one blow the drunk man not only knocked his wife out; he knocked Charrington clean out of business—for Charrington had nothing more to do with it.

There may be ways of making money which cost too much. In the choice of a profession or a trade, or in exercise of it, sometimes we have to ask ourselves, 'Can I do this and remember that God sees me do it?' That is the test which will decide if sacrifice is necessary or if, with a good conscience, we can go on.

(2) *We may have to give up comfort.* One of the first demands of the Kingdom is that we should realise our responsibilities to our fellow men. When John Wesley began life he had an income of £30 a year; he lived on £28 and gave £2 away. When his income rose to greater levels he continued to live on £28 and give the rest away. When a census of the silver in England was taken by the government, Wesley replied, 'I have two silver spoons, one in London and one in Bristol, and I am not likely to buy any more when so many around me lack bread.'

Our thoughts immediately turn to the incident of the Rich Young Ruler (Matthew 19:16-22; Mark 10:17-22; Luke 18:18-23). That tells how Jesus ordered a young man to sell all he had and give the proceeds to the poor. The question is, 'Is that injunction universally binding, or is it something which applied to the Rich Young Ruler personally and to people in like case?'

It so happens that there is another version of that story. It exists in a very early gospel called the Gospel according to the Hebrews of which only fragments remain. One of these fragments runs:

One of the rich men said to Jesus, 'Master what good thing am I to do that I may live?' He said to him, 'Man, obey the law and the prophets.' He replied, 'I have obeyed them.' He said to him, 'Go, sell all that you possess, and distribute it to the poor, and come and follow me.' But the rich man began to scratch his head and was displeased. And the Lord said to him, 'Why do you say I have obeyed the law and the prophets? For it is written in the law, Thou shalt love thy neighbour as thyself; and behold many of thy brothers, sons of Abraham, are clad in filth, dying of hunger, and thy house is full of many goods and absolutely nothing goes out of it to them.'

It was not the possession of riches which Jesus condemned; it was the selfish use of riches. Riches themselves are neutral; it is the use of them which matters. But we may well feel called upon to sacrifice our own comfort for the sake of others who do not have enough.

(3) *We may have to sacrifice family ties.* Jesus made it clear that the supreme loyalty must be to him. He told his disciples that they might have to abandon their nearest and dearest for his sake (Matthew 10:34-37). He was not asking anything that he himself had not been prepared to do. When he was beginning his ministry and it was becoming plain on what course he was set, his own friends and relations came and said of him, 'He is beside himself' (Mark 3:21). In the ancient world, over and over again, houses were divided and families split on the score of Christianity. That still happens on the mission field. For us it is not likely to happen in this blunt form, but it remains true that loyalty to Jesus must take precedence over every earthly attachment.

The Adventure

There leaps out in this parable the sheer adventure of Christianity. If everything is to be given up for the higher good, it follows that there is a certain element of sheer risk. To give up everything for the one pearl of great price is an action which even from the business point of view has a certain recklessness about it.

The Jewish Rabbis frequently inculcated this lesson of giving up things for a higher good. Here is one of their stories:

Rabbi Jochanan was going up from Tiberias to Sepphoris and he was leaning on the shoulder of Rabbi Chijjah ben Abba. They came to a field plot, and he said, 'This used to belong to me but I sold it to study the Law.' Rabbi Chijjah ben Abba began to weep. When he was asked why, he said, 'I weep because thou hast nothing left for thy old age.' He answered, 'Chijjah my son, it is a small thing in thine eyes that I sold something that was created in six days that in place thereof I might gain that which was given in forty days and forty nights?'

62

It is this truth which C H Dodd sees dominating the parable. He sees it against the immediate situation. The invitation of Jesus is, 'Follow me.' But it was abundantly clear that following him was a dangerous thing. The orthodox were against him; the Scribes, Pharisees and Rulers were out to eliminate him. His cause looked like a losing one. He seemed to be inviting men to face death. So in the parable he was saying, 'Are you willing to sacrifice everything, security, safety, comfort, possibly life, to follow me?' The willingness to risk is the price of entry to the Kingdom.

In this Jesus was far wiser than his followers in later ages. The tendency nowadays is to play down the difficulty of Christianity. The alleged ease of Christianity is offered as an inducement to its acceptance. In fact it is the lesson of all history that the opposite is the most effective.

There was the case of Pizarro, the famous Spanish explorer in South America. At as certain point he drew a line in the ground. He pointed out that on the north lay Mexico with it comparative safety and security; on the south lay Panama with all its dangers. 'Let each man choose,' he said, 'as befits a brave Castilian': and they flocked to take the harder but the more glorious way.

Shackleton tells how he advertised for volunteers for his South Pole expedition, for men to accept the threat of danger and death in snow and ice. To his amazement he was inundated with letters from volunteers in every walk of life. Men were coming in hordes for the privilege of a great adventure.

Studdert-Kennedy wrote a poem which tells of the crucifixion of Jesus and how the soldiers gambled for his clothes beneath the Cross. It continues:

He was a gambler too, my Christ,
He took His life and threw
It for a world redeemed.
And ere His agony was done,
Before the westering sun went down,
Crowning that day with its crimson crown,
He knew that He had won.

In the Middle Ages there was a company of men called the *parabolani*, which means 'the gamblers', They gambled with their lives. Where there was plague, where there was trouble, where there was risk, wherever a man might take his life in his hands to help others, they were there. Certainly it means unqualified risk to follow Jesus Christ. Few have accepted that risk.

11

Go Thou and do Likewise

Luke 10:25-37

A Dangerous Road

THIS is a story that tells of the kind of thing that frequently happened on the Jerusalem to Jericho road. It was a road notoriously dangerous for travellers. It might have been designed to suit brigands. Jerusalem, the city set on a hill, is 2300 feet above sea-level; and the road descended that 3600 feet in little more than twenty miles. It was therefore a road of sharp turnings and narrow defiles, which provided excellent lurking places for bandits.

A letter exists dated AD 171 in which a complaint is made to the government by two dealers in pigs. They too had fallen into the hands of brigands 'who assaulted us with very many stripes, wounding Pasion, robbed us of a pig and carried off Pasion's coat.' In the fifth century Jerome tells us that it was still called 'The Red or Bloody Way.' Even as late as the middle of the nineteenth century, travellers had to pay safety money to the local Sheiks if they wished to be safe from the attack of the Bedouin.

The grim history of the road extends even to our own time. The travel writer H V Morton, in his book *In the Steps of the Master,* writes:

When I told a friend that I intended to run down to the Dead Sea for the day he said, 'Well, be careful to get back before dark.' 'Why?' I asked. 'You might meet Abu Jildah ....' 'Who is Abu Jildah?' 'He is a brigand who has shot several policemen. There is a price of £250 on his head, and he has a habit of building a wall of stones across the Jericho road, stopping cars, robbing you, and, if you resist, shooting you. So take my tip and get back before dusk ....'

It would seem that, even by the early 1930s this very road was still a danger spot for the unwary traveller.

The Characters in the Story

Let us look now at the characters in the story.

(1) There was the *traveller*. One thing stands out about him—he was either very careless or very reckless, because seldom did any traveller venture on that road alone. Travellers almost always journeyed in convoys so that there might be too many of them for the brigands to attack.

(2) There was the *priest*. There were so many priests that they were divided into 24 *courses*. Each course served in the Temple for two separate weeks in the year. When they were not on duty many of them stayed in Jericho. The priest, according to the story, took one glance at the man and passed by on the other side. The Jews had all kinds of taboos. One was that anyone who touched a dead man was unclean for seven days (Numbers 19:11). That meant he could go about the ordinary business of life, but could not share in any religious service. Now for the priests in the different sections, their week of service in the Temple was the great event in their lives. It is most likely that the priest was genuinely sorry for the wounded man. But he was not willing to investigate whether he was dead or not; because if the man was dead and the priest touched his body, he would automatically be shut out from functioning as a priest in the Temple and his great week would be gone. The priest set the Temple ritual above the claims of humanity.

(3) There was the *Levite*. There is a subtle difference in his conduct. He apparently came over and looked at the man and then hurried past on the other side. There is one very probable explanation of this. It was a common thing for the bandits to use decoys. One of their number would act the part of a wounded man. When some unsuspecting traveller came by and stooped over the apparent victim, the rest of the band would suddenly rush from their concealment and catch him at every disadvantage. Perhaps the Levite had that in mind. He would have liked to help but the risk was too great.

And (4) then there was the *Samaritan*. The Samaritan was hated by the Jew. The quarrel between the Jews and the Samaritans had lasted for 450 years. Away back around 720 BC the Northern Kingdom, with its capital at Samaria, had been destroyed. Its inhabitants had been deported to Assyria and foreigners had been brought in. But it is always impossible to deport a whole nation and those who were left behind in time inter-married with the foreigners. By so doing they lost their racial purity and that was quite unforgivable in the eyes of the Southern Jews.

About 140 years later the same fate befell the Southern Kingdom whose capital was at Jerusalem. But these Jews even in Babylon kept alive their nationality and their religion, and abut 440 BC they were allowed to return under Ezra and Nehemiah and began to rebuild the shattered city and Temple. Immediately the Jews of the Northern Kingdom offered their help. It was contemptuously refused because, by their foreign marriages, they had lost the right to be regarded as Jews at all. Not unnaturally they were bitterly insulted and from that day there was bitter enmity between the Jews and the Samaritans (*cf* John 4:9). Therefore if this man is to be regarded as a racial Samaritan, no sooner would he be introduced into the story than the listeners would be sure that the villain had arrived on the scene.

But there are difficulties in regarding him as racially a Samaritan. He was clearly something in the nature of a commercial traveller. His visits to the inn were so regular that the innkeeper could depend on his coming back. The story implies that he had two animals with him, one on which he rode himself, and another on which he carried his packs. Now if this man was racially a Samaritan, what was he doing on the way either to or from Jerusalem? The Jews had no dealings with the Samaritans and it is so improbable as to be practically impossible that a Samaritan could have business in Jerusalem and could be obviously *persona grata* to a Jewish innkeeper.

There is a possible and simple explanation. In John 8:48 the rigidly orthodox Jews, shocked to the core of their being by Jesus' words and actions, said to him, 'Are we not right in saying that you are a Samaritan and have a demon?' The name *Samaritan* was used as a term of loathing and contempt for those who were law breakers and renegades from orthodox Jewish religion. If a man did not keep the ceremonial law, he was branded with the name of *Samaritan*. So most probably this commercial traveller was one of these people who were regarded with the gravest suspicion and dislike by the orthodox good people of the day; and the parable paints a picture of the orthodox passing by on the other side, while the despised heretic and sinner is the one man who helps his fellow.

Myself and my Neighbour

Of all Jesus' parables this might be said to be the most practical. It deals with the most practical of all problems and in the most practical way. It answers two questions.

(1) The question of the scribe was, 'Who is my neighbour?' and the answer of the parable is, 'Anyone who needs your help.' To the Jew this was startling. He felt a definite responsibility for his fellow Jew but none at all for the Gentile. The more stringent and less pleasant parts of the Sabbath Law, for instance, lay it down that if, on the Sabbath, a wall should collapse on a passer-by, enough may be cleared to see whether the injured man is Jew or Gentile. If he is a Jew he may be rescued; if a Gentile he must be left to suffer. Over and over again we pass by people in suffering and in need because, as we say, they have nothing to do with us. It is only when need comes to someone in our circle that we become active. Terence, the Roman poet, laid down a great law when he said, 'I count no human being a stranger.' There are some people whose instinct is to keep themselves to themselves; there are others whose instinct it is to help, and these have the spirit of Christ in them.

(2) Implicitly this parable answers the question, 'What is my duty to my neighbour in trouble?' And the answer is, 'Pity which issues in help.' Doubtless both the priest and the Levite felt a pang of pity for the injured traveller, but they did nothing to translate that pity into action.

In one of W J Locke's books there is a story about a man who had given his life to social service. One day, in conversation with a friend, the social worker complained:

When you see a fellow creature suffering and it shocks your refined sensibilities, and you say 'Poor devil,' and pass on, you think that you have pitied him. But you haven't. Pity, you think, is a passive virtue; but it isn't. If you really pity anyone you go mad to help him. You don't stand by with tears of sensibility running down your cheeks. You stretch out your hand because you have to.

The pity which remains merely an emotion is actually a sin, because it is always sin to experience high emotion and do nothing to turn it into action. Seneca, the Roman philosopher, said that what men wanted more than anything else was 'a hand let down to lift them up.' There is a story which seeks to make clear the different attitudes of the founders of the great religions to a man in trouble. A man had fallen into a pit and could not get out. Buddha passed by. 'Poor fellow,' he said. 'You must have been very foolish to get into a mess like that. I'm very sorry that I can do nothing to help you.' Mohammed passed by. He said, 'I am very sorry that I cannot get you out of the pit, but if ever you do get out I may be able to give you some advice which will keep you from falling in again.' Jesus of Nazareth passed by. He said nothing but got down into the pit and lifted the man out. Our duty to our neighbour is to reproduce the attitude of Christ, the attitude of an active pity whose hand is forever stretched out to help.

(3) Further, this parable lays down that practical service must take precedence in religion. The priest was so pre-occupied with the correct carrying out of the Temple service that he failed to respond to a fellow-creature's need. To him religion meant sacrifices must be absolutely properly made, that the incense must be meticulously burned, that the liturgy must be nobly correct. A Church may have all the dignity in the world and be quite dead, because true religion issues not in ritual and ceremony but in practical help for those who need it.

(4) The parable lays down that we must help even at risk to ourselves. The Levite frankly was unwilling to take the risk of helping the injured traveller lest he be involved himself. If a doctor refused

to attend a patient from whom he himself might catch infection, little healing would be carried out; but doctors nobly accept the risk. We may refuse to help because we do not want to get involved in any trouble; because, having nicely calculated the more and less, we come to the conclusion that if we help, we will have too little left for our own comfort; because possibly our motives may be misinterpreted. The true Christian counts the risk as less than nothing in comparison with the duty of helpfulness.

(5) Whether we take the Samaritan as racially a Samaritan or as a heretic and a loose-living man branded with that name of contempt, the fact emerges that there may be more real Christianity in someone with a hot heart and a stained record than in someone who is coldly and correctly orthodox.

I came through the centre of a big city late one evening. A young girl was following an unsteady course along the pavement because she was helplessly drunk. I carefully avoided her, embarrassed at the very thought of having anything to do with her. All the respectable people on the pavement did the same, looking at her with something between revulsion and contempt. Up to her came a man whom the respectable would have described as a tough citizen. He said to her, in the vernacular of his city, 'Where dae ye live, hen?' She told him in her fuddled way. 'Come oan, then,' he said, 'Ah'll tak' ye hame.'

The man who acted in a Christian way was the one whom orthodox Christians would have regarded askance. This parable lays down that the standard of judgment is not our respectability, but our willingness to help.

12

Even as I had Pity on Thee

Matthew 18:21-35

Peter's Question

THIS is one of the parables which springs directly from its context and whose context we possess. It all began with a question asked by Peter. He said to Jesus, 'If my brother sins against me and I forgive him seven times, will that do?' He obviously expected Jesus to say, 'Splendid, Peter! You could not possibly act more nobly than that.' After all, Peter had some kind of right to feel that he was doing well, for there was a Rabbinic saying, which said, 'If a man transgresses once, forgive him; if a second time, forgive him; if a third time, forgive him; if a fourth time, *do not forgive him.*' What Peter had done was to take the Rabbinic limit of forgiveness, multiply it by two, add one, and then sit back and say, 'Am I not a wonderful fellow to be willing to forgive like that?' Jesus put his answer in the form of this parable.

The Unforgiving Servant

The story is of a king who held a day of reckoning with his servants. He found that one owed him 10,000 talents. He was about to cast the servant into prison and sell his wife and family and all his goods. But in answer to the man's pathetic pleadings he forgave the debt and let him go. Immediately that servant went out and found a fellow servant who owed him 100 denarii. He would not listen to his request for time to pay, but threw him into prison until the debt should be discharged to the last penny. The other servants, enraged by the thankless justice of the whole transaction, told the king. The king sent for the servant and told him he should have forgiven others as he had been forgiven; and, because he had been merciless, treated him without mercy until the debt *he* owed was discharged.

The Unpayable Debt

The parable is full of vivid touches. Straight away there leaps out the contrast between the two sums of money involved.

The servant owed the king 10,000 talents, an enormous sum by the standards of the day. But the point is the completely unpayable nature of that debt. Something of its deliberate vastness can be seen from the fact that the annual taxation of the provinces of Judaea, Idumea and Samaria brought in a total of 600 talents; while that of Galilee and Perea amounted to 200 talents. The debt was more than the income of a whole group of provinces. It was quite beyond payment.

On the other hand, the debt which the fellow servant owed was comparatively trifling. The *denarius* was a Roman silver coin worth almost a shilling. The debt therefore amounted to, at the most, five pounds. So the man who had just been forgiven the unpayable debt of millions of pounds dealt mercilessly with a man who owed him a fiver.

A Different Standard for Others

There are two further interesting things about this servant's treatment of his fellow. He took him by the throat. The Roman and Greek practice was to grasp a debtor by the neck of his toga and rush him half-throttled to court; for quite often in the ancient world the plaintiff in a case made his own arrests. The Greeks talked about choking the life out of a debtor when they meant dragging him to court.

Perhaps even more interesting and significant is a point which does not emerge in the Authorised Version. In the Authorised Version the servant is made to say to his fellow servant, 'Pay *me* that thou owest' (Matthew 18:28). In the Greek there is no *me*. It is a perfectly general injunction—pay your debts. It is as if a long discussion was ended by the unforgiving servant saying self-righteously, 'Any honest man pays his debts.' There is something grimly humourous in the sight of a man who had just failed to pay a colossal debt which ran into millions, laying it down as a rule of life to a man who owed him a few pounds, that honest men pay their debts.

Let us deal with that last point first. One of the faults of the unforgiving servant was that he *demanded standards from others which he was not prepared to fulfil himself*. Of all human faults, this is the most common. We are often very critical of others and very easy with ourselves; often open-eyed to the faults of others and unwilling to see our own. What is candid frankness in us is discourteous brutality of speech in others. What is selfishness in others is standing on our indisputable rights in our own case. What is meanness in others is thrift in our own case. Should we fail in anything, we produce half a dozen valid reasons which in others would be feeble excuses. We should think more of Jesus' commandment to do to others as we would have them do to us. If we treated others with the same understanding charity with which we usually treat ourselves, it would be a happier world and there would be fewer breaches between us.

The Forgiving Spirit

But the main lesson of the parable is that we cannot receive the forgiveness of God until we have shown forgiveness to our fellow men. The parable may be said to be a commentary on two things which Jesus said. First, 'Blessed are the merciful for they shall obtain mercy' (Matthew 5:7). Second, 'Forgive us our debts as we have also forgiven our debtors' (Matthew 6:12).

It is true that at all times there have been great souls who say this duty of forgiveness. The Jews at their highest knew about it. In the apocryphal book of Ecclesiasticus there is a lovely passage.

Forgive thy neighbour the hurt that he hath done thee;
And then thy sins shall be pardoned when thou prayest.
Man cherisheth anger against man;
And doth he seek healing from the Lord?
Upon a man like himself hath he no mercy;
And doth he make supplication for his own sins?

(Ecclesiasticus 28:2-4)

One of the Rabbis laid down that there are four different types of character. 'First—he who is easily provoked and easily pacified; his loss is cancelled by his gain. Second—he who is hard to provoke and hard to pacify; his gain is cancelled by his loss. Third—he who is hard to provoke and easily pacified; he is a good man. Fourth—he who is easily provoked and hard to pacify—he is a wicked man.'

They knew that forgiveness is a lovely thing. And yet in actual practice it was not forgiveness which swayed them, but the desire for vengeance and the bitter heart. Undoubtedly when Jesus spoke about forgiving seventy times seven, his mind was glancing back to that grim old passage in Genesis 4:24 where it is not forgiveness but vengeance that is sought for seventy times seven.

As someone has put it, God's inflow of mercy to us must coincide with our outflow of mercy to others. The Lord's Prayer is very definite. 'Forgive us our debts as we also have forgiven our debtors.' In that petition we pray that God will forgive us *in proportion* to our own forgiveness of others. It follows that when we pray this prayer with bitterness in our hearts, with a quarrel still dividing us from someone else, we are deliberately asking God not to forgive us, because we have not forgiven others.

Every morning in his South Sea home, Robert Louis Stevenson used to conduct family worship. One morning in the middle of the Lord's Prayer he rose from his knees and left the room. His wife was alarmed because Stevenson was never well and she thought that he had taken suddenly ill. 'Is there anything the matter?' she asked, when she had followed him from the room. Stevenson answered, 'I am not fit to pray the Lord's Prayer today.' When we are in danger of unthinkingly rhyming off the prayer that Jesus taught us to pray, we would do well to stop and think if we are actually asking God not to forgive us; for we must forgive as we hope to be forgiven.

God's Forgiveness and Ours

Further, this parable, by its contrast between the colossal and unpayable debt which the servant owed the king, and the trifling sum which his fellow owed him, compels us to remember that any wrong which has been done to us is as nothing to the wrong which we have done to God.

When we disobey God, when we disregard him, when we banish him from life or any part of life, we are not so much sinning against law, as sinning against love. We are not breaking God's law so much as breaking God's heart. It is possible to pay some kind of legal penalty which will atone for a broken law, but it is impossible to do anything which can atone for a broken heart. Therefore, the debt we owe to God is infinitely greater than any debt anyone can owe to us.

That is what the real Christian cannot help seeing. Knowing that he himself has been forgiven so much, he cannot be unforgiving to any other person. The American Bryan Green tells of an incident in a mission he conducted. At the end of the mission he asked certain people to state in a few sentences just what this mission had done for them and what Christ now meant to them. One young girl rose and said, 'Through this mission I have found the love of Jesus Christ— and he has made me able to forgive the man who murdered my father.' That is an extreme case. But the fact remains that the person who has really appreciated what the love of God has done for him, cannot but love others and seek always to forgive as he has been forgiven.

The Mind of God

Why is there laid on the Christian not only the privilege of being forgiven but also the duty of forgiving. There is one basic reason. No one can enter into really close fellowship with another if he is his very opposite in mind and heart and spirit. It is possible to be close friends with someone, many of whose opinions we dislike, or with many of whose beliefs we disagree. But if our outlook on life is quite different there can be no real friendship and no real fellowship.

That applies to us and God. If we see things differently from the way in which God sees them, then there can be no fellowship between us and him. God's whole attitude is one of forgiving love. He sends his rain on the just and the unjust and makes the sun shine on the evil and the good. Out of his love he sent into the world his own son. Not only does he wait for men to come humbly and contritely asking forgiveness. In Jesus he goes to find them and offer them his love. If we are dominated by bitterness, if in our hearts there is a little chapel of hate, if we say, 'I can never forgive and I can never forget', then the principle of our life is diametrically opposed to the principle of the life of God. Therefore if we would enter into real fellowship with God, we must learn by his grace to forgive as he forgives.

13

A Certain Rich Man

Luke 16:19-31

Lazarus

THIS is the only one of Jesus' parables where any of the characters is given a proper name. Although custom calls the rich man *Dives*, which is Latin for 'rich', that name is not in the parable; but *Lazarus* is named. Why should that be? We cannot say for certain; but *Lazarus* is the Greek form of the Hebrew name *Eleazar*, which means, 'God is my help.' And the name may well be to emphasise the truth that even if the poor righteous man has no other helper, God is his help.

Dives and Lazarus

In the parable, detail after detail is added to stress the luxurious wealth of Dives and the abject poverty of Lazarus.

Purple and fine linen was the most costly of all clothing. The high priest's robes were made of purple and cost a colossal sum in those days. Dives 'feasted sumptuously every day': the word used means that Dives lived the life of a glutton, a gourmet and a sybarite. Oesterley makes a very interesting, relevant point here. He stressed the words *every day*. He points out that we quite unjustifiably limit the impact of the commandment concerning the Sabbath Day. The part of the commandment which we know and quote is, 'Remember the Sabbath day, to keep it holy; in it you shall not do any work.' But there is another part: 'Six days you shall labour.' This second part is just as valid as the first. The Jews glorified work. No Rabbi for instance might receive money for teaching. He had to have a trade in order to support himself. They had a saying that if a father did not teach his son to work, he taught him to steal. The commandment to work on six days was just as binding as the commandment to refrain from work on the seventh day. Therefore Dives, by his everyday way of life, was already branded as an utterly useless person, and a breaker of a positive commandment of God.

The parable goes on to describe Lazarus. The sores which covered him were terrible ulcers, so common in the east. He was so weak and defenceless that he could not even ward off the dogs who pestered him all the time. The Authorised Version says that Lazarus was laid at Dives' gate; but the Greek really means that he was thrown down there. The picture is of the friends of Lazarus carrying him grudgingly to the gate, impatiently throwing him down and hurrying away on their own affairs. The Authorised Version makes Lazarus wait for the crumbs which fell from the table of Dives. In the Greek there is no word for crumbs; it means simply the things which fell from the table. Montefiore, himself a Jew, tells us that in those days there was a very wasteful custom. Since there were no knives and forks and spoons, hands became quickly soiled; and in rich households it was the custom to place loaves of bread beside the guests. They wiped their hands on hunks of bread and flung the hunks away. It was most likely this that Lazarus was waiting for.

Dives and Lazarus after Death

As the life of Dives and Lazarus is contrasted, so is their fate after life. *To be in Abraham's bosom* was the phrase used to describe the highest bliss of Paradise. The picture is of Abraham dandling Lazarus on his knee as a mother might nurse a child. It was a common Jewish belief, and an even more common early Christian one, that Paradise and hell were in sight of each other, so that sight of the bliss of the blessed might intensify the suffering of the wicked; and sight of the suffering of the wicked might intensify the bliss of the blessed. In one picture of the life to come it is said that, 'He will deliver the wicked to the angels for punishment to execute vengeance on them because they have oppressed his children and his elect; and they shall be a spectacle for the righteous and the elect; they shall rejoice over them.' It is a grim thought that part of heaven's joy was to watch the sufferings of the sinner in hell. There was an old idea that even in hell the sinner can repent. If he did, then after a year Abraham would come and lead him to the blessedness. They said, 'When the godless have repented Abraham goes down into Gehinnom, he who kept all the commandments. He brings them out through his merits.'

The Life to come

This parable has certain great lessons to teach both regarding the life to come and the life of this world. We began by saying in the Introduction that it was dangerous to erect a theology on any one parable; and it would be wrong to extract a whole doctrine of the life to come from this one. But certain things do emerge.

(1) After death *identity* remains. In the world to come Dives was still Dives and Lazarus was still Lazarus. Different religions have had differing ideas about this. The Buddhist dreams of his Nirvana where he will cease to exist altogether. His idea is that existence of any kind is an evil and that heaven is achieved when existence is put off completely. The Stoics had what, at first sight, is a noble idea. They said that God was a fire, purer than any earthly fire. A man's soul was a spark of that divine fire, and, when life departed, the spark returned to the fire of which it was a part and was re-absorbed in God. Immortality to them was an absorption into the divine with the necessary loss of individual personality. But Christianity is clear that after death personality survives; that you will still be you, and I will still be me. This lays a terrible responsibility on us because it means that the only thing we take with us when we leave this earth is our *selves*.

(2) After death *memory* remains. The story implies that Dives was able to look back and see the life that he had lived. Surely in many cases that will be the very punishment we have to bear. When we look back and see things as God sees them, when we see the people we hurt and remember the things of which we are ashamed, that will be the sorest part to endure.

In Marlowe's play *Faustus*, Mephistopheles comes to Dr Faustus and Faustus asks what he is doing out of hell. He answers:

Why, this is hell, nor am I out of it.
Think'st thou that I, who saw the face of God
And tasted the eternal joys of heaven,
Am not tormented with ten thousand hells
In being depriv'd of everlasting bliss?

The essence of his hell was in the memory of what he had lost.

(3) After death *recognition* remains. The question is often asked whether or not we shall know our loved ones after death. Surely the answer is that heaven will not be heaven if we do not meet again those whom we have loved and lost awhile. Alexander Woolcott illustrated it thus: he imagined the arrival of J M Barrie in heaven; and then he painted a picture of Margaret Ogilvie, Barrie's mother, to whom Barrie owed everything, hiding as it were behind a pillar, too shy to step out, but the proudest woman in all heaven that day because her son is come.

Getting what we want

There are certain quite general points in this parable at which we must glance in the passing. It makes it clear that a man will get what he wants but that he must pay the price for getting it. Abraham said to Dives, 'You chose to set your heart on worldly things; now you must pay the price.' On the other hand Lazarus had set his hope and thought on God, as his very name shows; now he will have his reward.

We can get anything in this world if we are ready to pay the price for it, but in the end there are certain things which cost too much. George Macdonald tells of a village draper who grew rich by always keeping his thumb on the measure and giving his customers just a fraction too little. He says of him, 'He took his soul and put it in his siller bag.' The draper certainly grew rich, but it was at the expense of his soul. Dives had chosen what he wanted; now he had to pay the price. It is as if God said to us in this world, 'You can have whatever you want,' and our choice in itself led in the end to heaven or hell.

The Plea of Ignorance

Further the parable lays down that it is not possible for a man to plead ignorance in his own defence. When Dives asks for a special messenger to be sent to his brethren, the answer is that they already know what is right. As Denney said, 'If they do not learn sympathy with the Bible in their hands and Lazarus at their gates, not even a voice from the dead will teach it to them.'

There is a maxim in law which says that on occasion ignorance may be a defence; but *neglect of knowledge never is*. We may forgive a child for certain things, since he or she never had the chance to know any better; but a civilised adult cannot be forgiven: the adult knew or ought to have known. God has given us his Book, his Spirit in our hearts, the voice of conscience speaking within, the example of all good and godly men. If a man says that he did not know, it is the excuse of one who is at once a coward and a fool.

The Condemnation of Dives

In the end there remains one question about this parable which demands an answer. Why is Dives so uncompromisingly condemned? Rarely in all the gospel is someone so definitely consigned to hell. Dives was not obviously a bad or cruel man. He did not kick Lazarus in the passing; he did not order him to be removed from his gate; he seems even to have been perfectly willing that Lazarus should be fed with the hunks of wasted bread that fell from his table.

The sin of Dives was simply this—he accepted Lazarus as part of the landscape. He accepted the fact without question that he, Dives, should move in purple and fine linen and feast sumptuously every day, while Lazarus should lie, starving and full of sores, at his gate. He could look at Lazarus and feel no sword of pity pierce his heart. It never even dawned on him that it had anything to do with him.

In the 1860s a young man called Barnardo came from Dublin to London. He had heard God speaking to him, asking, 'Whom shall I send and who will go for us?' Barnardo's mind was set on being a medical missionary in China, for he desired to care for men's bodies as well as for their souls. In his little spare time he began a meeting for poor boys in the East End of London. After one of these meetings one lad would not go away. Repeatedly Barnardo urged Jim Jarvis to go home; and in the end Jim Jarvis made the simple statement that he had no home to go to. That night Barnardo learned a great deal about how the homeless waifs of the East End lived. But still his thoughts were set on China.

Shortly afterwards he met Lord Shaftesbury at a dinner party and told him about Jim Jarvis. Shaftesbury frankly refused to believe that it was possible. Barnardo said that he could prove it. He took Shaftesbury to a warehouse in Whitechapel. It was covered with great bales with tarpaulins over them. Barnardo put his hand in between two bales and pulled out a boy. When the boy was sure that Shaftesbury was a friend he said that he could produce another twenty lads at once. In a matter of minutes, from the corners and crannies of the warehouse, no fewer than 73 boys were assembled. So Shaftesbury saw; and one day, not long afterwards, he said to Barnardo, 'Are you sure that it is to China God is sending you?' And Barnardo suddenly knew that God was sending him to the homeless lads on his own doorstep.

All that happened in London in 1866. Up to that time many people had seen the situation but simply accepted it as part and parcel of the conditions of life. But there came this man Barnardo who felt the sword of pity pierce his heart and compel him to do something about it. Elizabeth Goudge wrote, 'It was not what Dives did do that got him into gaol; it was what he did not do that got him into hell.' Barnardo saw need and suffering and did something about it; of such is the Kingdom of Heaven. Dives saw it and did nothing; and he is the man who in all the New Testament is most uncompromisingly condemned.

14

God be Merciful

Luke 18:9-14

The Scene and the Characters

HERE again Jesus is surely telling a story from real life. The thing reads so vividly that it cannot be otherwise. It happened in the Temple Courts. There were four times of prayer—9 am, 12 midday, 3 pm and 6 pm; and the strict Jew was careful to observe each of them. To the Temple Courts went two men.

(1) The first man was a *Pharisee*. The name *Pharisee* literally means 'the separated one.' The Jewish scribes and Rabbis, beginning from the great principles of the Ten Commandments, had amplified the Jewish law until it included tens of thousands of petty regulations covering every moment and every action of life; and they considered that the keeping of these regulations was a matter of life and death.

As an example let us take the regulations governing the washing of hands. To eat food with unwashed hands was a grave sin leading to poverty and disaster. In general this is obviously a good healthy rule. But the hands had to be washed in a certain way. Water had to be specially kept. At least as much as a quarter of a *log* must be used, that is enough to fill one and a half egg-shells. The water was poured over both hands and each hand was cleansed by rubbing it with the fist of the other. Finally the hands were held up and the water must run the length of the wrist and then run off. Then the whole business was repeated, but this time the hands were held pointing down, and the water must run down to the finger tips. If anything was altered or omitted it was deadly sin.

No ordinary mortal could continue within the everyday business of life and observe all these regulations. So the Pharisees *separated* themselves off from the ordinary activities of life. But not only did they separate themselves off from the ordinary business of life; they cut themselves off from their fellow men as well. They considered it a matter of defilement to talk to, to do business with, to receive hospitality from, or give hospitality to, anyone who did not observe the law as meticulously as themselves. The almost inevitable consequence was that they acquired a haughty disdain for every ordinary person. It was not that the Pharisees were bad men. No one but men desperately in earnest would have made life so completely uncomfortable for themselves as they did; but they knew they were good and believed everyone else to be bad. The saying of a certain Rabbi Simeon reduces the whole thing almost to a parody: 'If there are only two righteous men in the world, I and my son are these two; if there is only one, I am he.'

So the Pharisee stood and prayed. There is nothing necessarily significant in the fact that he *stood,* because standing was the normal Jewish attitude for prayer; but if we read between the lines we can see that the Pharisee, to put it at its lowest, had no objection to being seen. When he did pray, he prayed *with himself.* Officially the prayer was a thanksgiving to God; in fact, it was an essay in self-congratulation. He was not really grateful to God, but he was exceptionally well pleased with himself. He thanked God that he was neither a robber, an unjust man or an adulterer. He went on to say that he fasted twice a week. Here he is telling God that he did far more than was necessary. The only obligatory fast among the Jews was on the day of Atonement. But people could, if they felt so disposed, fast on Mondays and Thursdays. These were the days of the midweek service in the Synagogue because Moses was supposed to have ascended Mount Sinai to receive the Law on a Monday and to have come back down on a Thursday. The Pharisee gave tithes of *all* his income; here again he is claiming credit for going beyond what is necessary. And above all he thanked God for not being like this tax collector. Altogether the Pharisee does not present a pretty picture. A man who is deliberately comparing himself with others to their disadvantage and his own advantage seldom does.

(2) The other character was the *tax collector.* Rome had a curious method of collecting taxes. Generally speaking she assessed an area at a certain sum and then let out the right to collect its taxes to the highest bidder. So long as the contractor paid to Rome the sum agreed, he

was free to keep the rest to himself. And since there were no ready means of spreading information in the days before newspapers, radio or television, few knew how much they were compelled to pay and the tax collector could make a handsome profit.

There were three taxes which every man must pay—a *poll tax* for the privilege of existing, a *land tax* which consisted of one tenth of the produce of his ground, either in cash or in kind, and *income tax* which was one per cent of his income. But the great sphere of opportunity for the tax collector was in what we would rather call *customs duties*. There was an import and an export tax on everything which came into and went out of the country. There was a tax for entering a walled town, a market or a harbour. There was a tax for crossing a bridge. There was a tax for using main roads, for possessing a cart, on each wheel of the cart and on the animal which drew it. The tax collectors could stop a man anywhere and make him undo his bundles and demand tax on this and that article in them. To make it worse, sometimes if the poor man could not pay, the tax collector would offer to advance him the money at a quite exorbitant rate of interest and so get him still further into his power. The crowning crime was that generally these tax collectors were Jews who had sold themselves into the hands of the Roman government in order to make profit out of the misfortunes of their fellow countrymen. Public opinion classed together robbers, murderers and tax collectors. Tacitus notes that once he saw a monument erected 'to an honest tax collector'—a unique phenomenon.

So then this tax collector must have been one of the most hated men in town. Any yet there must have been some spark of grace in him, for otherwise why was he there praying at all? He stood far off, overwhelmed by his own unworthiness. He would not even look up, but stood with downcast eyes and beat his breast. And he prayed the sinner's prayer, 'God be merciful to me, a sinner.' In Greek it is *the* sinner, as if the tax collector regarded himself as the sinner *par excellence*. Yet the extraordinary thing was that in the end this man who knew his own sin got nearer God than the Pharisee who was conscious of nothing but his own virtue.

Negative Goodness

We note one thing straight away about the Pharisee's goodness; it was *negative*. The things on which he congratulated himself were the things he did not do. Even his fasting and his tithes were really negative things because they consisted in giving things up. Now that is the reverse of true goodness.

We speak of Jesus' most famous commandment as the Golden Rule: 'Do unto others as you would have them do unto you.' The fact is that this rule existed in Judaism and in many other religions in its *negative* form—'Don't do to others what you do not want them to do to you.' In its negative form it is comparatively easy. It simply means that there are certain things which we refrain from doing; but in its positive form it means that we must go out of our way to be as kind to others as we would have them be to us. It is not so very difficult to refrain from doing things; but it is god-like to do things always in the spirit of love. The result is that the man whose religion consists in *not doing things* may be well pleased with himself; but the man whose religion involves *doing things* will always feel his own failure, because he will know that he has never fully succeeded in doing all he ought.

There are many people whose religion consists almost entirely of prohibitions. But at the end of the day God will not ask, 'What did you not do?' He will ask, 'What did you do?' We may say 'I never injured anyone,' but the question is 'What did we do to make others happier and their life easier?' A negative religion is only half a religion and leads to a negative life.

The True Humility

The great lesson of the parable is the necessity of humility. Humility is of the essence of greatness.

Rita Snowden tells of a party of tourists in Germany. They were being shown the room in which Beethoven had lived and worked and the very piano on which he had composed the 'Moonlight Sonata'. One of the tourists, a young American girl, sat down at the piano and played the first movement of the sonata. When she had finished the guide said, 'You will be interested to know that we had Paderewski himself as visitor here last week.' The girl said, 'And I'll bet he did just what I did; I'll bet he sat down and played the sonata.' 'No, madame,' said the guide, 'He did not. Everyone besought him to but he said, "Ah no! I am not worthy."' The self-confident girl would touch the notes Beethoven touched; the master musician was too humble to do so.

To the end of the day, when Thomas Hardy sent a poem for publication in the *London Times*, he enclosed a stamped addressed envelope for its return should it be rejected. The possibility of the rejection of a poem by Thomas Hardy is nothing short of incredible, but the great man was so humble that it seemed quite possible to him.

The Humility which leads to Knowledge

In two directions humility is supremely necessary. If we are ever to acquire knowledge we need humility; the person who knows it all already will never learn. Long ago Plato said, 'He is the wisest man who knows himself to be very ill-qualified for the attainment of wisdom.' Quintilian, the famous Roman teacher of rhetoric, once said of certain scholars of his day, 'They would doubtless have become excellent scholars if they had not been so fully persuaded of their own scholarship.' It was that great scientist Sir Isaac Newton, discoverer of the law of gravity, who said that we were all like children playing with pebbles on the shore, perhaps finding a pebble a little prettier than the others, while the great ocean of truth lay undiscovered before us. The man who will learn must take as his motto, 'Teach me', for only when he is humble enough to know his own ignorance will he begin to learn, and the more he knows, the more he will realise the extent of what he does not know.

The Humility which leads to God

If we are ever to know God, we have need of humility. Two things are necessary in real religion.

(1) First we need *a sense of our own inadequacy*. When people

D

complained to Abraham Lincoln that he wasted time in prayer, he answered, 'I would be the greatest fool on earth if I thought that I could carry the burdens which are laid upon me for one day without the help of one who is greater and wiser than I.' We need the realisation that we cannot cope with life by ourselves.

(2) We need *the sense of sin*. The astonishing thing is that it was the best of men who were most conscious of their own sin. Paul can write of himself that he is the foremost of sinners (1 Timothy 1:15). Francis of Assisi can say of himself, 'Nowhere is there a more wretched, a more miserable, a poorer creature than I.'

In fact in Paul there is a curious evolution of thought. In Galatians (1:1), which is perhaps the first of his letters, he can write of himself as 'Paul an apostle.' In 1 Corinthians 15:9, in the heyday of his work, he writes, 'I am the least of the apostles, unfit to be called an apostle.' In Ephesians 3:8, towards the end, he can speak of himself as being 'the very least of all the saints', and *saint* was the normal early Christian word for a member of the Church; and at the end, as we have seen, he speaks of himself as 'the foremost of sinners.' He begins by thinking of himself as an apostle; he goes on to think that he is not worthy of that great office; he goes on further to think of himself as the least of all the ordinary members of the Church; and finally he thinks of himself as the chief of sinners.

The reason is not hard to seek. The older he became, the nearer he came to Jesus Christ; and the nearer he came to Christ the more he saw the difference between himself and the Lord of all good life. The final cure for self-satisfaction is to set our life beside the life of Christ. Then there is no room for self-congratulation any more. It has been said that the gate to heaven is so low that no one can enter it except upon his knees. God gives grace to the humble, but he resists the proud.

15

In as much

Matthew 25:31-46

The New Principle

IT was a Jewish man who paid this parable the greatest compliment. Montefiore called it 'the noblest passage in the gospel', and went on to ask, 'How many deeds of charity and love, how many acts of sacrifice and devotion, have been accomplished in the last 1800 years by the remembrance of these words?'

This parable has become so woven into our religious thought that it has become the very centre of Christian faith and practice. To us it lays down a principle of judgment that has becomes a common-place; but to the Jews who heard it for the first time it must have been shatteringly surprising.

The Jew expected to be judged on two standards. First, if he had, or if he had not, kept the law. If he had carried out all the regulations of the law and had observed the Ten Commandments he felt com-pletely safe. Second, he expected preferential treatment because he was a Jew. He was quite sure that God would judge other nations with one standard and the Jews with another, and that a man, just because he was a Jew, would be to all intents and purposes exempt from judgment altogether. And now the listening crowds were presented with this completely new standard of judgment—that everything depended on our reaction to the needs of others.

All Simple Things

This parable is packed with truth for life and living. We must note that in every case the help given is in simple things. So often we ask our-selves, 'What can I do for others?'; and because we cannot give hundreds and thousands of pounds, because we cannot build a hospital or alter social conditions, we decide that we can do nothing. But one of the points of this parable lies in the fact that in every case quoted, the help given is the kind of help that any man can give.

This was no new outbreak in the teaching of Jesus. He had said the same before. 'Whoever gives you a cup of water to drink because you bear the name of Christ, will by no means lose his reward' (Mark 9:41). 'Whoever gives to one of these little ones even a cup of cold water because he is a disciple, truly, I say to you, he shall not lose his reward' (Matthew 10:42).

Mabel Shaw, a famous missionary, relates how she was telling her little Bantu children in Africa about giving a cup of water in the name of the 'Chief', as they had learned to call Jesus. They were tremendously interested because in a hot country a cup of cold water can be beyond price. Not long afterwards she was sitting on the verandah. Up the village street came a string of porters, obviously exhausted. They sank down wearily at the side of the road. And then something happened. These men were of another tribe; that could be seen from their clothes and from the way they wore their hair, and there was suspicion and often hostility between tribes. Out from the verandah came a little line of the 'babies', the children of primary age. Each one had on their head a water pot. They were obviously a little frightened, but just as obviously determined to see this thing through. They went out to the tired porters; they knelt before them and held up their water pots, 'We are the Chief's children,' they said, 'and we offer you a drink.' The astonished porters knelt in return, took the water and drank, and 'the babies' took to their heels. They came running in to Mabel Shaw. 'We have given,' they said, 'a thirsty man a drink in the name of the Chief.' In any ordinary village, had these men asked for a drink, they would have been told, 'You are not of our village; get water for yourself.' It was Christianity which bridged the gulf. And it is clear that the simple act of the Bantu 'babies' would do more to make Christianity real to these porters than any number of sermons.

Long Ago Mohammed said, 'What is charity?' And then he answered, 'Giving a thirsty man a drink, setting a lost one on the right road, smiling in your brother's face—these things are charity.' These are the kind of things that anyone can do, if he or she will. So often, because we can do nothing great, we do nothing at all, but there are kindnesses which anyone can do. To do them is to walk the Christian way and in the end to win the approval of the Master.

Unconscious Goodness

It is to be noted that the people praised in the parable never realised what they were doing. Their goodness was quite unconscious; their kindness, sympathy and generosity were quite spontaneous. Again this is Jesus' regular principle. He was critical of those who every time they do a good deed call out the Burgh Band. He said that, when we give something, even our left hand should not know what our right hand is doing.

At their best the Jews knew this. They had a saying that in the best kind of giving, the giver does not know to whom he is giving and the receiver does not know from whom he is receiving. There is a lovely story of an old saint who was offered a reward for all the good deeds he had done. His one request was that he might be given the power to do good things without knowing that he was doing them. And so it happened that his shadow which fell behind him brought help and healing to all.

Many people will do good if they know they are going to get something out of it. There are those who grimly compel themselves to go about doing some kind of good in the hope that some day in heaven they will get it back with interest. There are those who will do good for the sake of prestige. If the good they may do is to remain unknown it will probably remain undone; but if it is to appear at the head of a subscription list it probably will be done. Most common of all, there are those who expect to be thanked for all they do. If they confer a benefit on others they expect a proper measure of thanks; and if a certain fuss is not made over them they feel cheated and resentful and will not do it again. The basic mistake of all these people is the simple fact that they are not doing good for the sake of others, but for their own sakes. According to Jesus the really good are those who do good quite unconsciously.

It is told that Oberlin was once crossing the Alps and got caught in a terrible snowstorm. He was rescued by another traveller; when taken to safety he asked to know his rescuer's name, so that even if he would take no reward he might still pray for him. The rescuer would not tell him. After a long argument, the rescuer finished the matter. He said, 'Do you know the name of the good Samaritan in the parable?' 'No,' said Oberlin, 'scripture does not tell us that.' 'Well,' said the rescuer, 'there is no need for you to know mine.' Real goodness does not want its name mentioned. Its thrill is the thrill of seeing someone go more happily on his or her way.

If We had known

In the same way the defence of those who were condemned is suggestive. In effect they say, 'If we had known that it was you who was in trouble we would have helped quickly and eagerly enough.' There can be a certain snobbery in giving. Many a man would cheerfully give to some well-known person who happened to be in need, while he would never notice the need of some ordinary person. If he might select some nice, clean, guaranteed grateful beggars, that would be all right. But to give to all in need is a different kettle of fish.

Once a gushing and apparently pious lady came to Thomas Carlyle and asked him if he did not think that, if Christ were to come again, we would welcome him. Carlyle answered, 'Madame, if Christ had come well-dressed, and preaching doctrines palatable to the higher orders, I would have received from you a card to a drawing-room reception marked—"To meet our Saviour." If he had come preaching his sublime gospel and companying with publicans and sinners you would have said, "Take him to Newgate and hang him."' If Carlyle was right, that lady's spirit was exactly the spirit that is condemned in this parable. There is no selectivity in Christian charity. It gives because it is compelled to give to anyone in need.

Indiscriminate Charity

Immediately we are faced with a problem. Does this mean what is called *indiscriminate charity*? Within the limits of Christian common sense we believe it does. It is a common point of view to say, 'I will give to institutions and to societies where the money will be wisely and carefully used, but not to individuals where I may well be cheated and imposed upon.' The obvious difficulty about such an attitude is that, in any event, it would remove the personal element from giving altogether.

Things can happen. A beggar came to the door of a house and the householder practically chased him away. It was a wild, stormy night. Late in the night a visitor came to say that someone had collapsed at the gate of that house. A doctor was called. The stranger was dead and the doctor's verdict was that he had died of starvation and exposure. He was the beggar who a few hours before had asked for alms.

Surely in this matter it is the Christian point of view that we must be prepared to risk being swindled in order to help the one who deserves. The calculation of charity is not a Christian thing. God did not measure his love according to our deserts; Christ died for the sinner even more than he died for the good man.

The Principle of Judgment

We began by saying that in this parable, Jesus introduced an entirely new principle of judgment, our reaction to the needs of others. God will not some day ask us to recite the creed, or put us through an examination in scripture knowledge, or investigate the orthodoxy of our theology. The basic question is, 'What did you do to make life easier for others?' And that question is not based on the great contributions to human welfare which the newspapers report and the history books recount, but on our action and interaction upon the people with whom we come into contact every day.

It was inscribed on a certain mother's tombstone when she died, 'She made life easier.' It was a fine tribute both in the eyes of men and of God. Robertson Nicol tells somewhere of his father. He was a country minister and had a passion for books. He amassed no fewer that 17,000 volumes, stacked all over his manse. His young wife died after eight years of married life in which she may well have been starved to death that her husband might avidly feed on knowledge.

The children were neglected and Nicol wrote afterwards, 'I always feel that I was defrauded in my youth—there was so little sunshine in it—far too little.' Here was a man who was a scholar, who could have taken a high place in any theological examination. But few will dare to say that he was a good man; and few will hold all the knowledge he brought to God an adequate substitute for his neglect of his family. This parable asks not 'What do you *know*?', but 'What do you *do*?'

In as much

Jesus' principle is summed up in the sentence, 'As you did it to one of the least of these my brethren, you did it to me.' When you come to think of it, that is inevitable on the basis of Jesus' teaching. He taught that God was Father; therefore all of us, whether we know it or not, are the offspring of God. Now in human life the best way to please a parent is to do something for his or her child. Parents are usually more grateful for something that is done for their son or daughter than themselves. It is not otherwise with God. In one sense we can *do* nothing for God and can *give* nothing to God, for God, being God, has everything. But surely we can do something for someone who is *a son or daughter of God*; and therefore the best way we can do things for God is by doing something for others around us: it is literally true that when we do something for others, something is done for God.

There is an old legend about Martin of Tours, the soldier saint. One cold winter day he was entering a city and a beggar asked for alms. Martin had nothing to give him. But the beggar was blue with cold and Martin took off the old battered soldier's cloak he wore, cut it in two and gave half to the beggar, who blessed him and was gone. That night Martin had a dream. In it he saw heaven and all the hosts of heaven; and Jesus, in the heavenly place, was wearing half a Roman soldier's cloak. One of the angels said to Jesus: 'Master, why are you wearing that old cloak?' And Jesus answered, 'My servant Martin gave it to me.'

16

How much more
Luke 11:5-8; Luke 18:1-7

The Friend at Midnight

WE take these two parables together because together they tell us certain very valuable things about prayer. The first, usually called the Parable of the Friend at Midnight, becomes much more vivid when set in its actual background. A man had an unexpected visitor late at night. Perhaps the visitor had miscalculated the length of his journey. Perhaps he had taken too long a siesta. In any event he arrived very late. The householder was worried because he had no food to set before him. That was quite natural. Jewish mothers baked their own bread and they baked only enough to last one day, so that there would be no waste. But in the East hospitality is a sacred duty; and it was not enough to set before a man a bare sufficiency of food. The guest, however unexpected, must be confronted with an abundance.

So the householder, late as it was, went down the street to borrow bread from a neighbour; but he found the door shut with the bar in its socket. That was a sign that the neighbour did not want to be disturbed. In Palestine life was very public. First thing in the morning the door was opened and anyone might go out and in; but if the door was shut, that was a sign that privacy was required, and no one would invade that privacy except for the most urgent reasons. But the householder was determined to get his loaves and he knocked.

It is little wonder that the neighbour was at first very unwilling to rise. The house of the Palestinian peasant consisted of one room. Two thirds of it was on ground level. The floor was simply beaten earth covered with dried reeds and rushes; and into that part very often the family live-stock were brought at night to keep them safe from robbers. At the top end of the single room there was a raised part like a low platform. On it burned the charcoal stove around which the whole family slept. Families were large in Palestine, for there was a curious belief that the Messiah would not come until all souls that should be born had been born. So to have a large family was to hasten the coming of the Messiah. All this made for warmth, but it was inevitable that if anyone rose at night the whole family was disturbed. So the householder at first refused point blank to get up. The Authorized Version speaks of the would-be borrower's 'importunity.' The word really means 'shamelessness.' The borrower was so eager to get the loaves that he did not care how much of a nuisance he made of himself; so he kept on battering at the door until at last the man in bed was badgered into getting up in sheer despair, for, by this time, the whole family was awake. So by his shameless persistence the borrower got his loaves.

The Unjust Judge

For the moment let us go on to the Parable of the Unjust Judge. It tells of a widow who had some case which she wished settled. In her village was a judge who had no respect either for God or man. He must have been a Roman judge because under Jewish law one man could not constitute a court. What usually happened was that the plaintiff chose an arbitrator, and the defendant chose another, and then a third was appointed who would act as chairman and have the casting vote. These Roman stipendiary magistrates were famous for their addiction to bribes. It was said of them that they would pervert justice for a dish of meat. There was no hope of extracting justice from them unless the requisite bribe was forthcoming.

B T D Smith quotes a passage from Tristram's book on *Eastern Customs in Bible Lands,* which shows that Jesus did not tell a made up story, but the kind of thing that could well happen.

> It was in the ancient city of Nisibis in Mesopotamia. Immediately on entering the city on one side there stood the prison with its barred windows through which the prisoners thrust their arms and begged for alms. Opposite was a large open hall, the court of justice of the place. On a slightly raised dais at the far end sat the *kadi* or judge, half buried in cushions. Round him squatted various

secretaries and notables. The populace crowded into the rest of the hall, a dozen voices clamouring at once that his cause should be heard first. The more prudent litigants joined not in the fray but held whispered communications with the secretaries, passing bribes, euphemistically called fees, into the hands of one or the other. When the greed of the underlings was satisfied one of them would whisper to the *kadi* who would promptly call such and such a case. It seemed to be taken for granted that ordinarily justice would go to the litigant who had bid the highest. But meanwhile a poor woman on the edge of the crowd constantly interrupted the proceedings with cries for justice. She was sternly bidden to be silent and reproachfully told that she came there crying out every day. 'And so I will,' she cried out, 'until the *kadi* hears me.' At length at the end of a suit the judge impatiently demanded, 'What does that woman want?' Her story was soon told. Her only son had been taken for a soldier and she had been left alone and could not till her piece of ground. Yet the tax-collector had forced her to pay the impost from which she, a lone widow, should be exempt. The judge asked a few questions and said, 'Let her be exempt.' Thus her perseverance was rewarded. Had she had money to fee a clerk she might have been excused long before.

There we have a real life parallel to the parable. The widow came to the unjust judge and kept on coming only to be rebuffed each time. But her persistence was wearing the judge down. In the end he decided to settle her case lest, as the Authorized Version states, she *wearied* him. The translation *wearies* is inadequate. It can mean one of two things. J A Findlay suggests that it means that the judge was afraid that he would lose 'face', which is so important in the East. But in ordinary colloquial Greek the word means 'to bruise someone's face' and was the word meaning 'to give someone a black eye.' It is by far the most likely interpretation that the judge decided to settle the case before the woman resorted to physical violence; so for her persistence the woman got the justice she desired.

Persistence in Prayer

Very often these two parables are used to inculcate the lesson of persistence in prayer. The idea is that if we batter at God's door long enough, in the end his resistance will be broken down and we will get what we want. There is a certain truth there. Oesterley makes the point in this way. Why, he asks, should God answer prayer, or even notice it, unless the proof is there that the prayer is offered in sincerity and in earnestness? And that can be shown only by persistence. 'In every other sphere the goal must be reached by energising, persistent effort; should not that be so in the greatest of all strivings?' Undoubtedly there is a truth there. But it is not the whole truth.

How much more

Luke tells the story of the Friend at Midnight and then goes on to relate that Jesus said something else:

> And I tell you, ask, and it will be given you; seek, and you will find; knock, and it will be opened to you. For everyone who asks receives; and he who seeks finds; and to him who knocks it will be opened. What father among you, if his son asks for a fish, will instead of a fish give him a serpent; or if he asks for an egg, will give him a scorpion? If you then, who are evil, know how to give good gifts to your children, *how much more* will the heavenly Father give the Holy Spirit to those who ask him!
>
> (Luke 11:9-13)

he whole point of these two parables is made in that phrase *how much more*. The point is not the *likeness*, but the *contract* between God and mankind. The parables say to us, 'If a churlish householder can finally be badgered into getting up and meeting his friend's need, if an unjust judge can finally be pestered into giving a widow justice, how much more will God as your loving Father give you all things that are needful?' The prime lesson is not that shameless persistence painfully extracts blessings from an unwilling God; but that, in prayer, we are coming to one who is our Father and who is even more ready to give than we are to ask.

The Laws of Prayer

But we cannot leave the matter there. The question immediately arises, 'Is it then true that I need only ask for what I want and I will get it from this loving, generous God?' There is much more to be said than that. There are certain laws in prayer.

(1) *God knows far better than we do what is good for us.* Over and over again a child asks from his parents things which would only hurt him or her. Many children wish to play with matches or push paper into the fire, and are stormily disappointed when stopped from doing so. Many desire to eat things which can only be a source of future trouble. A parent often has to refuse a child's request not because he does not love him, but because he does. God is in the same relation to us. We often find out, when we take the long view, that, had our prayers been answered, it would have been not to our good but to our harm.

(2) *God alone sees all time.* We are rather like someone who arrives at the cinema in the middle of the film. We have not seen the beginning—and we will not see the end. We can see only the little bit at which we are present. So, very often we pray in ignorance, and God does not answer the prayer in our way but in his, because he has something better in store for us.

In the days of Charles I, Oliver Cromwell and Richard Hampden were so tired of life in a country where there was no freedom that they decided to emigrate. They were actually on board ship when word came from the King that they must stay in England. They stepped ashore *bitterly disappointed*; but the fact was that in being prevented from doing the thing they wished at that moment to do, they were able to fulfil a far greater destiny.

(3) *Prayer must be absolutely sincere.* The persistence of the people in the parable was proof of the utter earnestness of their desires. It is quite possible to pray for things because they are the right things and yet not to want them. In fact, sometimes we would be

unpleasantly surprised if our prayers were literally answered.

In his later days Augustine was one of the greatest figures in the Christian Church; but when he was young he lived a very unsatisfactory life. When he was good he was wishing to be bad; and when he was bad he was wishing to be good. He tells us how he used to pray, 'O God, make me pure; make me pure.' And then he would add in a whisper, 'but not yet, but not yet.' He was praying for something he did not really want and he knew it. In prayer we must be sincere. If we know a thing is right but do not want it ourselves, we must pray God to help us really to desire it. We must desire an answer with out whole hearts before we receive it.

(4) *The effective prayer must be definite.* Luther used to say that usually we are far too vague in our prayers. It is not enough to say to God, 'O God, I am a wretched, miserable sinner.' We must detail our sins, really and definitely and often painfully, confessing them to God. That is particularly true when we pray to God for things we want. It is a great test of their rightness or wrongness, to see whether or not we can speak about them to God.

(5) *Our co-operation is absolutely essential.* We must pray and then do our best to make our prayers come true. It is always wrong to look on God as the easy way out. Suppose we are to sit an examination and we have done none of the work. We go into the examination hall, pick up the paper, read it and see that we do not know the answer to anything because we have been shirking when we should have been working. Suppose then we pray to God that we may pass this examination. Such prayer has no chance of being answered. But, if we entered the examination hall fully prepared and then found that we were so nervous that we could not do ourselves justice, we might then pray to God to keep us calm and that prayer would be answered because we had done our part first. No one would hope for a cure from a doctor unless he or she were prepared to co-operate with the doctor, to abstain from certain things, to take certain medicines, to undergo a certain discipline. When we pray for the poor to be helped, or for the sad to be comforted, or for the sick to be encouraged, our prayer is sadly ineffective unless we do what we can to help the very people for whom we pray. It is true that without God we can do

nothing; but God needs our help to make our prayers come true.

(6) When we remember God's love and God's wisdom, we see that there is one perfect prayer. After we have made our prayers to God, we must add, as Jesus himself added, '*Not my will, but thine be done.*' For the best prayer of all is not that which tries to extract things from God, but that which seeks to make itself always willing to accept what God in his love and wisdom sends.

17

Thou Fool!

Luke 12:13-21

Old yet ever New

HERE is a story which is as old as time and as new as today. It is the story of a man for whom life was one long success. He made his plan to enjoy himself in his own way and, suddenly, when everything seemed set fair, death intervened. It is the kind of story that occurs in all literatures. In Ecclesiasticus there is a passage like this.

There is that waxeth rich by his wariness and pinching,
And this is the portion of his reward;
When he saith, I have found rest,
And now will I eat of my goods;
Yet he knoweth not what time shall pass,
and he shall leave them to others, and die.

(Ecclesiaticus 11:18,19)

There is even an almost startling parallel from *Arabian Nights*:

A king had gathered together a vast store of gold and other treasures and had built for himself a great palace reaching the sky. One day he ordered a feast to be prepared for his court, and sitting on his throne he communed with himself saying, 'O soul, thou hast heaped up for thyself all the good things of the world; now give thyself up to them and enjoy these treasures in a long and happy life.' Scarce had he finished when the angel of death came for him.

When Jesus told this story, he told of something which happens in every age and generation.

The Circumstances of the Story

This is one of the parables which spring directly from their context. It was the usual thing that people came to respected Rabbis with their problems. The fact that the man in the crowd came to Jesus with his problem is an indication that Jesus was regarded as a Rabbi and held in respect.

In point of fact the man had no real problem. His request was that Jesus should speak to his brother about the division of the estate, presumably of his father. Jewish law was quite definite. The law was that the eldest got two-thirds and one-third was given to the younger son, or divided amongst the younger sons. Therefore there was no question about the division of the estate. This man knew the law well enough but he was not satisfied with his share. He was a covetous creature who sought to inveigle Jesus into siding with his covetousness. That is why Jesus begins with his warning about covetousness and then goes on to tell his vivid story.

The Rich Fool

It is usually call the Parable of the Rich Fool. There was a man, said Jesus, who had enjoyed a run of unbroken prosperity. So prosperous was he that his barns could not hold his crops. His solution was to pull down his barns and build bigger ones and then to sit back and enjoy himself for many years to come. Then God told him that his soul would be required of him that very night and his plans were shattered for ever.

A Warning to Us

The rich fool is held up as a warning to us. Let us see if we can discover just where he went wrong. We should note *the things he remembered and the things he forgot.*

Remembering the Wrong Things

First, the things he remembered:

(1) *He remembered himself.* It has been pointed out that there was never a soliloquy so full of the first person singular as the soliloquy of this rich fool. He asked himself, 'What shall *I* do because *I* have no room to bestow my fruits?' He goes on to say to himself, 'This will *I* do; *I* will pull down my barns and build greater and there will *I* bestow all *my* fruits and *my* goods.' From that he goes on to plan a life which apparently had not even the remotest thought for anything else except his own ease and enjoyment. To himself, he was by far the most important person in all the world.

It has been said that Jesus came to banish the words '*I*' and '*mine*' from life and to substitute '*we*' and '*ours*'. It is certainly significant that in the Lord's Prayer the first person singular never occurs; it is always the first person plural. Self is banished and man is taught to think of himself as one of a community of brethren.

The ancient monks in the Egyptian desert may have made many mistakes in their outlook on life, but they had one very lovely custom. It was laid down that no monk might ever speak of '*my*' book, '*my*' pen, '*my*' cell; and to use the word was regarded as a fault demanding rebuke and discipline.

So often it is precisely the other way. Rita Snowden tells how someone remarked on a self-centred lady, 'Edith lived in a little world, bounded on the north, south, east and west by Edith.' This parable is the final condemnation of the man to whom the most important word in the English language is '*I*'.

(2) *He remembered this world.* The rich fool never had a thought for anything except the world in which he was living. He had got himself so thirled to it that, as far as he was concerned, no other world existed. There is such a thing as an other-worldly Christianity which despises this world. For that there is nothing to be said. But it is possible to swing right round to the other direction and to worship this world. Boswell tells how Dr Johnson, after being shown through a vast estate and a magnificent castle, remarked, 'These are the things which make it difficult to die.'

The idea of such a person is to amass things which, he believes, can ensure happiness and security. That is a hopeless task. The Jews had a saying, 'Who so craveth wealth is like a man who drinks sea water. The more he drinks the more he increases his thirst and he ceases not to drink until he perishes.' There is an unwritten saying of Jesus, 'The world is a bridge. The wise man will pass over it but will not build his house upon it.' He meant that the world is of first rate importance, but that it is a stage to another world: he who forgets that has really forgotten the main object of life.

Forgetting the Essential Things.

Now, the things which the rich fool forgot:

(1) *He forgot his neighbours.* If his barns were too small to hold his crops, there must have been many who would have been only too glad to share in his surplus. If he had only looked around him he could have found many ways of disposing of the too much that he had. Nowhere is this more clearly seen than in his idea of enjoyment. His notion of happiness was to take his ease, to eat, to drink. His one thought was to have a good time. One of the greatest tests of a man is, where does he find his enjoyment? Does he connect enjoyment entirely with himself? Or does he connect enjoyment with making other people happy? If he seeks solely selfish enjoyment he will not get it. The author Barrie summed it up: 'Those who bring sunshine into the lives of others cannot keep it from their own.'

(2) *He forgot time.* The whole attitude of this man was that he had unlimited time. Now, it is one of the features of all great men that they have been impressed, sometimes even obsessed, with the shortness of time. Andrew Marvell could always hear 'time's wingèd chariot hurrying near.' Keats had *'fears that I may cease to be, Before my pen has glean'd my teeming brain.'* Robert Louis Stevenson wrote:

The morning drum-call on my eager ear
Thrills unforgotten yet; the morning dew
Lies yet undried along my field of noon.

But now I pause at whiles in what I do,
And count the bell, and tremble lest I hear
(My work untrimmed) the sunset gun too soon.

C E Montague tells how he first realised the urgency of time. He heard a sermon from Jowett, the Master of Balliol. In it Jowett said, 'I find it set down in tables that the average duration of human life at the end of 21 is 36 years. We may hope for a little more; we may fear a little less, but speaking generally 36 years or about 13 000 days is the term in which our task must be accomplished.' It was the reduction of the matter to days which struck Montague; and there came to him the utter certainty that not one of these days could be wasted by any honourable man.

Again, there is a famous saying of Dr Thomas Chalmers. When he was a young parish minister in Kilmany, he spent five days a week lecturing on Mathematics in the University of St Andrews, and he said quite openly that one day a week was ample to discharge the duties and meet the needs of a country parish. He later found out how wrong he was, but once in the General Assembly it was thrown in his face that he had said this very thing. He admitted it and said that it had been done in the days of his ignorance. Then he went on, 'What is the object of mathematical science? Magnitude and proportion of magnitudes. But then, sir, I had forgotten two magnitudes. I thought not of the littleness of time; I recklessly thought not of the greatness of eternity.' Here again you have a man who, when he discovered the real essence of Christianity, discovered also the shortness of time.

It may well be said that the most dangerous word in the English language is the word *tomorrow*. It may be a grim thought, but it is a necessary one, that we have no bond on time. No one knows if for him or her tomorrow will ever come. There is an old story of three apprentice devils who were coming from hell to earth to serve their time. They were telling Satan before they left what they proposed to do. One said, 'I will tell men that there is no God.' 'That,' said Satan, 'will not do, because in their heart of hearts they know there is.' 'Well, I will tell men,' said the second, 'that there is no hell.' 'That,' said Satan, 'is still more hopeless, for even in life they have experienced the remorse of hell.' 'I will tell men,' said the third, 'that there is no hurry.' 'Go,' said Satan, 'tell them that and you will ruin them by the million.'

The rich fool forgot time. It is told of Alexander the Great that at every feast he kept a little model of a skeleton on the table beside him to remind him that, even at its happiest, time was short and death must come. It is a thing that all must remember, not simply as a grim and frightening thing, but as a challenge to prepare ourselves for taking a step to a greater work and a higher world and a life in the presence of God.

(3) *The rich fool forgot God.* As the proverb says, 'Man proposes; but God disposes.' There are some wise and warning verses in the letter of James. 'Come now, you who say, "Today or tomorrow we will go into such and such a town and spend a year there and trade and get gain"; Whereas you do not know about tomorrow. What is your life? For you are a mist that appears for a little time, and then vanishes. Instead you ought to say, "If the Lord wills, we shall live and we shall do this or that"' (James 4:13-15). The man who makes plans and leaves out God has left out the most important factor of all.

(4) *And the rich fool forgot that a man is what he is and not what he has.* He concentrated on the pursuit of the things he was bound to leave behind and forgot the things he could take with him. As the Spanish proverb grimly points out, 'There are no pockets in a shroud.' Or as we say, 'Sow a deed, reap a habit; sow a habit, reap a character; sow a character, reap a destiny.' In the last analysis the one thing a man can take with him when he leaves this world is himself. Alexander the Great gave instructions that when he died his body should be placed in the coffin in such a way that it should be seen that his hands were empty. The conqueror of the world was well aware that he could take none of his conquests with him. The supreme aim of life should not be the acquisition of merely temporary things, but the formation of a character which some day we may take without shame to God.

18

If it bear Fruit—well

Luke 13:6-9

The Invaluable Fig Tree

THE fig tree was the most valuable of all trees. It was naturally very productive and bore three crops within the year. It was in fact normally in fruit for ten months in the year, April and May being the only two months when figs were not to be found upon its branches. For this very reason it was common to find fig trees among the vines. The fig trees were much more certain than the vines and were a stand-by should the vines fail. Normally a fig tree did not fruit for the first three years. The point of the parable is that the master had waited the requisite three years for the tree to fruit; at the end of that period it was still unproductive and so he wished to cut it down. But the vine-dresser pleaded for another chance which would be the last chance of all.

The Immediate Meaning of the Parable

Undoubtedly the parable had an immediate meaning for those Jews who heard it for the first time. For them it meant that with Jesus the time of final opportunity had come. That is a note which occurs in the New Testament again and again. It sounds in the preaching of John the Baptist. 'Even now the axe is laid to the root of the trees; every tree therefore that does not bear good fruit is cut down and thrown into the fire' (Matthew 3:10; *cf* Luke 3:9). It was John's belief that, with the coming of Jesus, an hour of destiny had come. Jesus himself said the same thing:

> The men of Nineveh will arise at the judgment with this genera-
> tion and condemn it; for they repented at the preaching of Jonah,
> and behold, something greater than Jonah is here. The queen of
> the South will arise at the judgment with this generation and

condemn it; for she came from the ends of the earth to hear the wisdom of Solomon, and behold, something greater than Solomon is here.

(Matthew 12:41,42)

To the people of Israel had come chance after chance to hear the voice and accept the offer of God. It had come with the Law of Moses; it had come in the long line of the prophets; and now it had come in the Son of God. Just as the fig tree was to receive one last chance, Israel was to receive one final opportunity to take God's way. The coming of Jesus was a last chance, for the simple reason that God could do no more. It was impossible for God to make a more urgent or moving appeal than the very sending of his Son. To reject him was finally to reject God, because beyond him God's appeal could not go.

Uselessness invites Disaster

While that was the immediate lesson of the parable, it nevertheless contains many other general lessons. It teaches us that *uselessness invites disaster*. Because the fig tree was useless it was threatened with destruction. The ultimate test of any one is, 'Of what use is he or she in the world to God?' Let us again be quite clear about this. To be useful does not necessarily mean doing 'great' things. It is quite possible to be of the greatest use by doing what look like little things.

The Revd Alexander Whyte had a favourite story. A commercial traveller called Rigby used to travel regularly to Edinburgh. Now Rigby was no preacher; in fact he found it hard to talk of religion at all; but he always attended Whyte's church St George's on Sunday, and before he left the hotel he always invited someone to come to church with him. One Sunday morning he invited a man and at first the man angrily refused; but Rigby persisted and finally the man went. He was so impressed with Whyte's preaching that in the evening he asked Rigby to go with him again. At that evening service something happened to the man who had at first refused to go. He decided to become a Christian.

Next morning business took Rigby past Whyte's house. He had

109

never met Whyte, but on the impulse of the moment he knocked and asked to see him. He told Whyte what had happened the day before. Whyte said, 'God bless you for telling me. I thought Sunday night's sermon fell flat and I was very depressed about it.' And then Whyte went on, 'I didn't quite catch your name. What is it?' 'Rigby,' he said. 'Man, I've been looking for you for years!' He went into his study and came back with a bundle of letters. He read one. It began, 'I was spending a weekend in Edinburgh and a fellow-commercial called Rigby invited me to come with him to St George's; and the service that day changed my life.' Every letter in the bundle was the same. And Whyte went on to say, 'Out of that bundle twelve came from young men, and of those twelve, *four have already entered the ministry.*' It does not seem a great deal to invite someone to come to church, and yet what infinite use to God were the invitations of that man called Rigby.

It can be even simpler than that. When God wants something done and someone helped he has to find a hand to supply that help. Often it may be the simplest of simple things. Robert Browning's wife wrote a poem in which she described two girls who worked as seamstresses. One was off her work ill; the other at once set out to go to her even if it meant losing her pay and perhaps her job. 'God has a missing hand this minute,' she said. 'Lucy wants a drink perhaps. Let others miss me—never miss me, God.' By doing the simple things we are of use. By being of service in the ordinary everyday things, we in the end serve God.

A Cumberer of the Ground

Further, the barren fig tree risked destruction because *it was a cumberer of the ground.* It was taking up space which might have been given to something useful; and it was using up nourishment without making any return. Here we come, perhaps indirectly, but quite definitely, across one of the most fundamental aspects of Jesus' teachings about life. For Jesus goodness was always a positive thing. One of the most common claims is, 'I never did any harm to anyone', and the person who says that seems to think he has established his claim to be reasonably good. The demand of Jesus is not, 'Have you done no harm?' but 'What good have you done?' The basic sin is to take more out of life than we put in.

It may be that we *have* to do that because we are in debt to so many people for their kindness and goodness to us. So we may put it in another way: even if we must be a debtor to life, then the basic sin is not to *try* to repay that debt we owe. The Christian test is not 'What did you *get out of* life?', but 'What did you *put into* life?' George Bernard Shaw said, 'I am of the opinion that my life belongs to the whole community. And so long as I live, it is my privilege to do for it whatever I can. I want to be thoroughly used up when I die, for the harder I work the more I live.' We are living in a world where the tendency is to try to extract more and more reward for less and less work; and at its basis this is not an economic problem at all, but a moral and religious one. Nearly all the problems of the world's work would be solved if men and women everywhere attempted the Christian duty of putting more into life than they take out.

The Greatest of all Failures

Still further, the fig tree was in danger of destruction because it was guilty of the greatest of all failures: *the failure to realise its own possibilities*. It had it in its nature to be the most prolific of all trees. In this particular case it had a very special chance because it was fortunate enough to be planted in a vineyard. It was in fact fruitless; therefore it was in danger of condemnation.

The most common word for sin in the New Testament is the Greek word *hamartia. Hamartia* is a shooting word and it means a failure to hit the target. Charles Lamb tells of a man called Samuel le Grice. In his life there were three stages. When he was young, people said of him, 'He will do something.' As he grew older, they said of him, 'He could do something if he tried.' And towards the end they said of him, 'He might have done something if he had wanted to.' That precisely is *hamartia,* and that is *sin.* To have some ability and to make nothing of it, to have been able to make some contribution to life and not to have made it, to have been able to have

111

rendered some help and not to have rendered it, that is sin. God does not ask us to do more than we can; but he does demand that we act up to the limit of our capabilities and in loyalty to the highest that we know.

The Fig Tree's Champion

One thing is still to be noted. Even when it had failed, *the fig tree found a champion.* The vine-dresser secured for it another chance because he believed that it was capable still of realising its destiny.

Jesus is our champion. The most significant thing about him is his tremendous belief in us. That is proved beyond all doubt by the height of the commands he gave. No leader ever expected more from his followers. He obviously believes us capable of the highest goodness and of the greatest heroism. And he believes that, even after we have let him down.

The great example is Peter. No one can ever have hurt Jesus so much as Peter did, and yet when he rose from the dead Jesus sent a special message to Peter to tell him that he still believed in him (Mark 16:7). The very fact that Jesus believes in us should fill us with a new determination not to fail him. We hear of an army captain, loved and respected by all his soldiers, and we are told, 'He looked at us and we looked at him; and then we determined to be what he believed us to be.' When we think of how Jesus believes in us, it must be the great aim of life to justify that belief.

The Limit

There remains one thing more, and it is a stern thing. *There is a limit.* After one year more, the limit for the fig tree came. For us too there is a final chance.

It is the law of life that those who fails to use a faculty will lose it. Those who live long enough in the dark will become blind. Those who refuse to use an arm or a leg for a period of time will find the muscles will atrophy and paralysis will set in. Those who always read cheap books will lose the ability to enjoy good books. Those who always listen to inferior music will ultimately be unable to appreciate good music. And those who consistently refuse the invitation and challenge of Christ can in the end make themselves totally incapable of accepting it. It is not God who has condemned those people; they have condemned themselves.

So in the end this is a parable which tells us that so long as we keep on trying to follow Christ, however inadequately, we are never shut out; but, when we refuse to make the effort, we can shut ourselves out.

19

And the Door was Shut

Matthew 25:1-13

The Marriage Feast

THERE were three stages leading to marriage:

(1) *There was the engagement.* This was usually carried out by the parents or by professional match-makers. At this stage the couple might be mere children and probably would never even have seen each other. This custom still exists among the Jews. Pure-blooded Jews are increasingly rare and a family may search for a bridegroom of untainted heritage for their daughter and a marriage may be arranged before the couple have even set eyes on each other. The strange thing is that this way does in practice produce happy marriages.

(2) *There was the betrothal.* This happened when the couple were approaching marriageable age. It was carried out with feasting and ceremony almost as elaborate as the marriage itself. It was absolutely binding and could not be broken except by divorce. If the man died the girl was technically a widow.

(3) One year after that, came *the marriage proper*. It was a time of great joy. Everyone joined in the festival and in the procession to the home of the newly-married couple. 'Everyone,' says a Jewish saying, 'from six to sixty will follow the marriage drum.' Even the Rabbis left the studies to which they were so devoted because marriage was something given by God. The point of this parable depends on a marriage custom which to us may seem strange. The couple did not go away but stayed at home for what we could call their honeymoon. The week following the marriage was one continuous feast when the couple held court; they were actually called and were treated like king and queen. It was the opportunity to share in that week of glad festivity that the foolish virgins lost.

The picture of the girls waiting for the bridegroom was the kind of thing that happened and still happens. If the bridegroom came from any distance there was no saying when he would come; and since he was a supremely honoured guest, not to welcome him when he did come was a serious breach of manners.

Dr J Alexander Findlay recounts his own experience in Palestine:

The Parable of the Bridesmaids begins with a picture which is stamped upon my memory, because when we were approaching the gates of a Galilaean town, I caught sight of ten maidens gaily clad and playing some kind of musical instrument as they danced along the road in front of our car; when I asked what they were doing, the dragoman told me that they were going to keep the bride company till her bridegroom arrived. I asked him if there was any chance of seeing the wedding, but he shook his head, saying in effect, 'It might be tonight, or tomorrow night, or in a fortnight's time; nobody ever knows for certain.' Then he went on to explain that one of the great things to do, if you could, at a middle-class wedding among townsfolk in Palestine was to catch the bridal party napping. So the bridegroom comes unexpectedly, and sometimes in the middle of the night; it was true that he is required by public opinion to send a man along the street to shout, 'Behold! the bridegroom is coming!' but that may happen at any time, so the bridal party have to be ready to go out into the street to meet him whenever he chooses to come .... Other important points are that no one is allowed in the streets after dark without a lighted lamp, and also that, when the bridegroom has once arrived, and the door has been shut, late-comers to the ceremony are not admitted.

And so the ancient customs continue to this very day. In the parable the ten virgins were awaiting the arrival of the bridegroom. They did not know when he would come. Those who were wise were prepared for his coming no matter when it happened. Those who were foolish let their oil run down and were caught unprepared. The lamps were rags soaked in oil and the oil needed to be replenished. While they sought to remedy their omission, the door was shut and they were shut out.

The most interesting parallel of all is quoted by Oesterley from a traveller's account of a personal experience in India:

The bridegroom came from a distant city, and the bride dwelt in Serampore, whither he journeyed by water. After a wait of from two to three hours it was at last announced as midnight approached —precisely in the words of Holy Writ—'Behold the bridegroom! Come forth to meet him!' All those taking part in the ceremony lighted their lamps, and carrying them in their hands, hastened to take their places in the procession. But some of them had mislaid their lamps, and were not prepared to take their places; but it was now too late to go and find their lamps; and the procession moved on to the house of the bride. The company then entered into a large, beautifully illuminated courtyard. The bridegroom, borne on the arms of his friends, was placed in a gorgeous seat in the centre of the assembly. Very soon after he entered into the house, and the d shut behind him, and guarded by sepoys. I and others, desiring to enter, appealed to the watchman at the door; but in vain. Never was I so struck by the realism of our Lord's beautiful parable as in the moment when 'the door was shut.'

It may well be that when we hear this story first there is an element of cruelty in it to our western ears; but it relates an incident which must have been commonplace and which simply reflects the everyday life and customs of the people among whom Jesus lived and taught.

To the Jews

To the Jews who heard this parable for the first time it had a very special significance. If ever a people should have been ready for the full display of God's truth, it was they. Throughout the centuries God had been preparing them as his people; and yet when his Son came they refused him and in the end crucified him. Because they did that they shut themselves out from the Kingdom. Now, it was nobody's fault but their own. God had done everything to open the door to them and they had shut it on themselves.

The Necessity of being prepared

But there are wide and wise lessons here for every generation. First and foremost the parable teaches *the necessity of being prepared*. It is simply not possible to get ready certain things at the last minute. Unless they have been prepared long beforehand, they cannot be prepared at all. It is that way, for instance, with knowledge. The moment of the examination cannot be the moment of preparation. It is that way with all the skills of life.

The important thing always is knowing how to do it; and that knowledge is not something which can be acquired at the last minute. It must have been stored up long ago. That is why the time of youth must be the time of learning. We are told that it is almost impossible to learn anything new after the age of thirty. That is an exaggeration, but the fact remains that the golden age of memory is from seven to eleven; the younger we are, the more easily we learn. There are things that we will never learn at all unless we learn them when we are young.

The Lost Opportunity

Again, we must be ready to seize the opportunity when it comes. Perhaps we have heard the story of the understudy who, when the principal player fell ill, went on stage and was received as a great success; or of a reserve player who, due to the illness of a first team player, was given a marvellous opportunity and seized it with both hands. But the fact is that the understudy did not leave it until that moment to learn the part; the reserve did not leave it until that moment to be trained to the last ounce of strength. By diligent preparation both were ready to seize the chance when it came.

If that is so of the ordinary things of life, it is still more true of the great things. The greatest event of all is that some day we will stand in the presence of God. For that we must make ourselves ready. It is told of an old Scotsman that, when he was dying, someone offered to read the Bible to him. To their surprise he did not seem very eager for this, although they knew that all his life he had nourished his heart and his mind on God's book. They asked him why. His answer was, 'Ah theekit ma hoose when the weather was warm.' In other words, he had thatched his house in the calm weather and now he was ready. It is told of Mary of Orange that when she was dying her chaplain came to speak to her about the things of eternity. 'My friend,' she answered gently, 'I did not leave this matter till this hour.' It is the sensible thing to have things ready for every emergency and for the greatest emergency of all.

Things which cannot be borrowed

Further, this parable lays down that *there are certain things which cannot be borrowed.* The oil could not be borrowed in the moment of necessity. There are two things of supreme importance which cannot be borrowed

(1) *Faith cannot be borrowed.* A common charge is laid against our generation—that we are living on the spiritual capital of our fathers. What is meant is this. We want the world to be a place where human life is respected, where virtue is honoured, where women and children are safe, where men obey the law of God. But what are we doing to keep it so? We cannot have a world like that without, for instance, a strong Church. Are we pulling our weight within the Church? We cannot have a world like that without men of prayer who live close to God. Are we making ourselves into such men and women? We owe the good in the world to our forefathers; we live on their spiritual capital; but it is our plain duty to maintain that heritage and not simply to live on it.

But there is something more personal than that. It may be that the heritage it has received will go far to keep the world in the right way. But when we are faced with some overmastering temptation, or some difficult task, we cannot conquer that temptation or shoulder that task in someone else's strength. We must do so in our own. It is then our plain duty to build up a faith which is our own faith and which cannot be shaken.

(2) *We cannot borrow character.* It is pleasant to depend on others. But some things are just not borrowable. When it comes to living life, we have to live it with ourselves as we are. What makes this doubly important is that in the end character is all we can take with us from this world; and the only character we can take is our own.

The Door was shut

The Jews had a proverb: 'A door that is shut is not so easily opened.' We must have a care that we do not shut doors upon ourselves. John Greenleaf Whittier, the American Quaker poet, wrote: 'For all sad words of tongue or pen, The saddest are these: *It might have been.*' We must ever be on the watch lest we let slip the opportunities to win the things we ought to have and to be the people we ought to be.

20

God Forbid!

Matthew 21:33-44; Mark 12:1-11; Luke 20:9-18

A Well-remembered Story

THIS is one of the few full-length parables related in all three Synoptic gospels. That in itself shows the deep and lasting impression it must have made. In one sense it is a parable of defiance, for in it Jesus faces his own fate, and at the same time utters to those who would kill him a threat which they could not fail to understand. Often we fail to realise the almost reckless defiance which Jesus displayed when he came to Jerusalem for the last time. Throughout those final days, so far from courting security and remaining prudently in the background, he seemed deliberately to focus the attention of all upon himself.

First, there came the Triumphal Entry (Luke 19:28-40). The significance of that episode is often lost to us, for the picture of Jesus riding on an ass produces the wrong effect on our western mind. In Palestine the ass was not a despised animal but a noble beast. Only in battle did kings ride upon a horse; when they came in peace they came riding upon an ass. The Triumphal Entry was a deliberately dramatised claim to be king. Then when he entered the city he proceeded to do what was literally the most shocking thing that ever he did. He cleansed the Temple, driving out the money-changers and the sellers of doves. Such an act could not be anything else but a sensation and must have set everyone talking (Luke 19: 45,46). It was little wonder that the priests and the scribes came to him saying, 'Tell us by what authority you do these things?' (Luke 20:1,2).

It was out of just such a situation that this parable arose. By this time it was clear that Jesus was going to die, and he was going to his death, not like a hunted criminal, and not apologetically, but like a king.

An Ancient Picture and a Modern Story

Jesus used two things in this story:

(1) He used one of the most ancient symbols for the nation of Israel. The picture of the nation of Israel as the vineyard of God was an old picture. Its most famous occurrence is in Isaiah 5:1-7. No one who heard this parable would be in any doubt that it was the nation about which he was speaking.

(2) He used a situation which in his day was common. Palestine was a troubled land and absentee landlords were numerous. It was by no means unusual for a man to let out his ground and go and stay in some more comfortable country. When that was done the rent was paid in one of three ways. It might be either a fixed sum of money, or an agreed proportion of the crop, or a definite amount of produce irrespective of what the crop was. Now at this time, as so often, Palestine was in a highly explosive state. There was unrest and labour troubles. And this very kind of thing could and did happen. Husbandmen did refuse to pay the rents, did beat up the absentee landlord's representatives and did resort to violence to gain possession of estates which were not rightfully theirs. This was a perfectly recognisable story.

The Meaning of the Parable

We said at the beginning that the parables of Jesus must not be treated as allegories; but in *this* parable every detail has a meaning. The vineyard is the people of Israel; the master of the vineyard is God; the husbandmen are the priests and the rulers who have controlled the affairs of Israel; the servants who were sent and ill-treated are the prophets whom God sent in every age and who were sometimes disregarded and sometimes martyred; the son is Jesus himself. So then this parable gives a vivid picture of God's care for Israel. His long patient pleading with his people, Israel continual rejection of God's way, the coming of Jesus, the death of Jesus, and finally his ultimate triumph and the final discomfiture of his enemies, who thought they had eliminated him.

Human Privilege

Certain points stand out clearly in this parable. First, it stresses *human privilege*. In Matthew it is clear that everything possible was done for the vineyard. It was hedged round about so that marauding animals could not gain entry. The wine press, a great stone-lined pit in the earth, had been dug so that the grapes could be pressed and the juice extracted. A watch tower had been built so that sentinels could keep guard against robbers (Matthew 21: 33). Just so, all through history everything had been done for the nation of Israel that they might be ready to recognise God's Son when he came; and yet in spite of their privileges they failed entirely.

One of the supreme tests of life is, 'How did we use our privileges?' Oscar Wilde has a terrible kind of parable like this. Jesus was walking through the streets of a city. In an open courtyard, he saw a young man feasting gluttonously and growing drunk with wine. 'Young man,' said Jesus, 'why do you live like that?' 'I was a leper and you cleansed me. How else should I live?' Jesus went on, and he saw a young girl clad in tawdry finery, a girl of the streets, and after her came a young man with eyes like a hunter. 'Young man,' said Jesus, 'why do you look at that girl like that?' 'I was blind,' said the young man, 'and you opened my eyes. How else should I look?' 'Daughter,' said Jesus to the girl, 'why do you live like that?' 'I was a sinner,' she said, 'and you forgave me. How else should I live?' Here were three people who had received priceless gifts from Jesus and who failed to use them to the good.

We live in an age which has had every privilege. We have good homes, a Christian country, freedom of worship, a Church to be our mother in the faith, parents who gave us every chance. We live in an age which has discovered more of the secrets of power than any other age. How then are we using our privileges? Remember, we are answerable for the privileges we have received.

Human Freedom

Further, this parable stresses *human freedom*. It is significant that after the master had let out the vineyard he went away into another country (Matthew 21:33; Mark 12:1; Luke 20:9). It was as if he said, 'I have given you this job and this responsibility; now I am not going to interfere; run it your own way.'

The argument regarding fate and free-will is an old one in which the debate continues. It may be that on strictly logical grounds it is insoluble; but the fact remains that the instinct of man is that he is free. Every time we criticise someone we assume that he might have acted otherwise. Every time we feel regret or remorse it is because we feel that we might have taken some more honourable course of action. There can be no such thing as goodness if we are not free. Goodness lies in the choice between the higher and the lower thing.

Someone has laid down the difference between fate and destiny —fate is what we are compelled to do; destiny is what we are meant to do. We have a destiny but we are not fated. And what we are meant to do is to put ourselves on God's side within the world. Toscanini was once rehearsing an orchestra which was not really trying. Quietly he laid aside his baton and said, 'Gentlemen, God has told me how he wants this piece of music played; and you—you hinder God.' So we have the freedom of being for or against God.

Sin is deliberate

Inevitably this leads to the conclusion that *sin is deliberate*. There are three theories of sin which eradicate the deliberate element in it.

(1) *Sin is merely traces of our ancestry.* Man has climbed up from a time when he was nearer the beasts. With him he has taken certain relics of the lower things. If then we sin, we are not really responsible for it. Give men time, says this theory, and they will outgrow their sins as a child outgrows bad habits. The unfortunate thing for that theory is that it collapses against the facts; for the fact is that the higher man reaches in knowledge and power, the more terrible his sins and their consequences become.

(2) *Sin is undeveloped good.* This theory would say that man's sins are either undeveloped good, or good things which have somehow gone wrong. A weed is a flower that has gone astray. The courage and

skill of, let us say a cat burglar, are good qualities misused. It is then argued that sin can be eradicated by a process of education. But the facts are against this theory too. At a time when education is stressed as never before, lawlessness is as rife as ever. Education cannot change the essential man, although it may succeed in changing him from being merely a devil into being a clever devil, which is worse.

(3) Sin is a physical matter of glands and of constitution. Therefore man is not responsible for it, because if he happens to be made that way he cannot do anything about it. This theory clashes with the Christian conception of man, for man is not a body only. He is body, mind and spirit, and the greatness of Christianity often lies precisely in the fact that it enables us to conquer the things of the body by the power of the things of the soul.

This parable lays down that sin is the deliberate action of man in disobedience to the known will of God.

The Patience of God

This parable lays down still more *the patience of God*. The master of the vineyard was not content with one invitation. He gave the husbandmen chance after chance to mend their ways. The patience of God is the most wonderful of all things. When we consider the matter dispassionately and from the human angle, we are bound to wonder that God did not destroy the world long ago. In other words, if God had been a man with human reactions, he would long ago have smashed the universe to bits in sheer despair at our sins and follies. In a book by Israel Zangwill, the Jewish writer, one of the characters says that for her it is not the peace of God, but the *pain* of God, that passes understanding.

The Claim of Jesus

Further this parable stresses *the claim of Jesus*. Quite deliberately h removes himself from the level of those who had gone before. The prophets who had gone before are servants; but he is the well loved son. The message of the prophets was partial and fragmentary

(Hebrews 1:1). He is the fullness of God's revelation to men. It is never enough to think of Jesus as only a man, not even as the greatest of men. Once Napoleon was in a group of men discussing Jesus. The men were prepared to allow that Jesus ranked as the greatest of all men. Napoleon said nothing until the end, then he who had commanded many armies and known many men said simply, 'I know men and I know this—Jesus Christ is not only a man.' When we come face to face with the claims of Jesus our reaction must be unquestioning obedience to the one person who has the right to speak.

Final Rejection

This parable sets forth the grim possibility of *final rejection*. As we have seen again and again, after entering the world himself in the person of Jesus, God can do nothing more. If people remain unmoved by the life and death of Jesus, there is no further appeal. Jesus is, as it were, the touchstone of God, and by our reaction to him we are finally judged.

The Lost Task

There is one last lesson in this parable. All three accounts agree that the vineyard was to be taken away from those who had it and given to others (Matthew 21:41; Mark 12:9; Luke 20:16). Behind this lies the warning that the great task which should have belonged to the Jews had been taken from them and given to the Gentiles. The Jews should have been the nation to lead all men to God. Instead they rejected God's Son when he came; and so the task of evangelising the world had to pass to the Gentiles whom they despised. One of the most humiliating things in the world is to be given a real task by someone whom we respect and love, and then to find that, due to our weakness and foolishness, we have failed in our task and let down the person who trusted us with it. We will live well if the only thing we fear in this world is to fail God and let him down.

21

The Children of this World
Luke 16:1-12

A Strange Story

IN many ways this is the most puzzling parable Jesus ever told. First of all let us simply look at the story. A master had a steward who had complete control of his possessions. This was quite common. The master, though wealthy, probably could neither read nor write and he entrusted the management of his estate to the steward. Very likely the master was a money-lender and such loans were paid just as often in kind as they were in cash.

Here then we have a steward in absolute control of a rich, but uneducated, master's affairs. The steward used his position to carry out a policy of theft. Rumours arose and in due time these rumours reached his master's ears. He immediately called the steward to account, and he had no defence. This was a very grave situation for the steward. In spite of his position of trust and responsibility, he was a slave and dismissal would be instant. He would be left without a job; obviously no one else was likely to employ a man who had stolen from his master; and starvation seemed to stare him in the face.

So the steward set out to mend matters as far as he could; it is to be remembered that he along knew what was going on the business. He went to one man who owed 100 measures of oil. The measure in question is a *bath*, which was equal to almost five gallons. He told him to take his agreement and to change the amount to 50 measures, thus wiping out half the debt with a stroke of the pen. He told another who owed 100 measures of wheat to alter it to 80. The measure here is a *cor*, which was equal to slightly more than eight bushels. By so doing he calculated to win the gratitude of these debtors. He may have had further schemes. He may well have intended to shut their mouths as witnesses against him by involving them in his own dishonesty, and it is by no means impossible that he saw also the prospect of a little judicious blackmail after he had lost his job. The master got to know about it and, with a cynical appreciation of what we would call a very fast bit of work, congratulated him.

The Sons of this World and the Sons of Light

It is no easy task to find out just what this parable means. Luke himself found it difficult, for he attached no fewer than three different lessons to the parable. The first lesson is found in verse 8. 'The sons of this world are wiser in their generation than the sons of light.' What does Luke mean?

We must note that the parable deals with the machinations of a set of rascals. The steward was obviously a rascal and a quick-witted one at that. He had pilfered from his master's business, and he proposed to escape the consequences of one misdemeanour by plunging into a series of others. The debtors were obviously quite content to be dishonest and to alter their agreements as fast as they could if they could get away with it. The parable ushers on to the stage a set of extremely unsatisfactory characters.

But they were wholehearted in their rascality. The steward was willing to make every effort to maintain his comfort. The debtors were willing to catch at any chance to cancel part of their debt. If Christians were as keen on their Christianity as these men were on their dubious business, it would be a vastly different world. As Hugh Martin said, 'If they took as much trouble with their Christianity as they do in trying to reduce their handicap at golf or in growing their roses they would be much better people.'

We may easily test ourselves in this matter. How much time do we give to our work, our hobbies, our sports, our outside interests? And how much time in comparison do we give to the things of religion? How much of our day is spent in amusement and how much in prayer, in meditation and in the reading of God's word? Is it the case that the weather may serve as a reason for not going to church while the same weather would never deter us from a sporting spectacle or an expedition to some occasion of pleasure? In this parable, if this is its interpretation, Jesus is saying, 'Look at the way the worldly rascal works for the things he values; if you would work at your Christianity with the same enthusiasm, you would be much better people.' It is entirely probable that this *is* the lesson of the parable; but let us look now at the other lessons which Luke attaches to it.

Friends of the Mammon of Unrighteousness

The second lesson which Luke attaches to this parable is in verse 9: 'Make friends for yourselves by means of unrighteous mammon, so that when it fails they may receive you into the eternal habitations.' In the New Testament *mammon* stands for all material things on which men set their hearts. So then this means, 'Use your material possessions to make friends for yourself, so that in the day of trouble you may reap the benefit of these friendships, just as the steward used his control of money to make friends for himself.'

There are three basic attitudes which a man may take up towards money.

(1) He may regard money as *an enemy*. He may refuse to have anything to do with it. That is what the hermits of the desert did. They absolutely refused to possess anything. They regarded all material things as so tainted that no Christian person could handle them. That is obviously a wrong attitude for, if it were universally adopted, the whole structure of life would break down. The hermits depended on the charity of others; but if all had been like themselves, there would have been no one to give charity.

One thing proves that Jesus was not like that. Jesus was thirty when he set out upon his mission for God along the roads of Palestine (Luke 3:23). What had he been dong all these thirty years? *He had been the village carpenter of Nazareth.* Many scholars believe that Joseph died young and that Jesus took upon himself the support of the family at Nazareth and kept it on his own shoulders until his younger brothers had grown up enough to take on the business. There is in fact a legend that he made the best ox yokes in all Galilee and that, from all over the country, people came to buy the yokes that Jesus made. Village shops in Palestine had their signs swinging over the doors and it has been suggested that the sign over the shop of Jesus the carpenter of Nazareth was, 'My yokes are easy' (cf Matthew 11:30). The Greek word for *easy* can also mean *well-fitting*. Jesus was so conscientious in business that he never made an ill-fitting yoke which might gall the shoulders of the patient oxen. Jesus accepted the problems of serving the public and of making a living. He would never have dismissed material things as things with which a man must have nothing whatever to do.

(2) He may regard money as *a master*. That is to say, he may be the slave of money. That is the case of the miser, or of the man whose one desire is to make money and who does not care how he makes it. He may be making it by methods which are dishonest or are the ruin of other people. But he does not care so long as he gets it. We do well to remember when we are thinking of how to get money, that money can cost too much.

(3) He may regard money *as a friend*. That is to say, he may use it wisely and unselfishly. In that case he will do good both to himself and to others. A man's conduct of his money affairs is a good test of himself. Dr Boreham tells of a meeting at which Christian people were describing their religious experiences. One woman sat silent. She was asked to speak but refused. From the look on her face it was easy to see that something was badly wrong. When asked what the matter was, she answered that more than one of the people who had just made glowing testimonies to Christ owed her money—and her family was near to starving. There could be no sincerity in testimonies like that. If we use material things rightly we will neither worship them nor despise them, but use them to bring strength, beauty and comfort to our own lives and to the lives of others.

Fidelity

But Luke adds a third lesson to this parable in verses 10-12. The essence is in the first phrase, 'He who is faithful in a very little is faithful also in much.' If this be the lesson of the parable, then it means that if we show ourselves untrustworthy, as the steward did, no one will trust us. Levison tells us of just such a case, of a steward who acted like the steward in the parable and who was dismissed. He set up in business for himself; but from that time no one would trust him and he died in the most wretched poverty. There is no virtue on which God and men set such store as fidelity, and no fault which so condemns a man as untrustworthiness.

The young Calvin Coolidge had a characteristic that he took with him when long afterwards he became president of the United States. His father often had to go to town and he left instructions with Calvin about things that ought to be done before he came back. When he returned he never looked to see if these things had been done; he knew that he could rely absolutely on Calvin to do them. It is servants like that that both God and men always need.

22

Yet there is Room
Matthew 22:1-10; Luke 14:15-24

The Great Feast

LUKE'S version of this parable is far more straightforward than Matthew's. In Matthew's version two alien verses (6 and 7) have somehow strayed in. They tell of a war against a city; and even in a parable, where the details are not to be stressed, a king could hardly carry out a war of vengeance while the feast was all ready and waiting. These two verses are very likely part of a similar parable. If they are omitted the story in Matthew reads straight through and is almost exactly like that of Luke.

The story is of a householder who prepared a great feast. The procedure may seem strange to us, but in Palestine it was normal. If a man purposed to hold a banquet, he fixed the day ahead but not the exact hour. When the day came, the more honoured guests were personally summoned by servants sent to fetch them. Those not so summoned divided themselves into two classes. Those who had no great opinion of their own importance were there early, humbly grateful for the invitation and determined not to miss it; those who had a good opinion of themselves waited until the last minute, or actually came late, to made an entry and let everyone see that they were there.

The Reluctant Guests

When the day came, a servant was sent out to summon the guests and they all began to make excuses. One had bought a field and had to go and see it; another had bought some new oxen and was keen try them out; another was newly married and refused to leave his wife. Now, not to provide adequate hospitality was a grave discourtesy, but to *refuse* offered hospitality was a deliberate insult. So the host took steps to fill the empty places at the banquet. He sent out his servant to call in the under-privileged from the streets and back lanes of the city. If the invited would not come, then some who perhaps never in their lives had had the chance to sit at a banquet must become guests. Even then there was room, and the highways and hedges were combed to find people to enjoy the munificent hospitality of the master. A joy such as they had never expected entered into the lives of many; but those who should have been the guests missed a chance which would never return.

The Banquet of God

The idea of a great banquet given by God was a thoroughly Jewish idea. The Jews believed that when the Messiah came and the new age dawned, one great event would be a banquet at which all sat down. Jesus took over that old idea and used it; that he did so is extremely significant. We must note that Jesus compared the Kingdom of Heaven to a *feast*. A feast is an occasion of joy. Clearly Jesus thought of the Kingdom as a happy thing. To enter the Kingdom was as joyous a thing as to go to a banquet. It would have been well if Christians had always remembered that. Too often the charge against Christianity has been that it took all the light, zest and joy out of life. Men have too often seen Christianity as that which made them do all the things they did not want to do and abandon all the things they would have liked to do.

The hermits in the desert deliberately courted discomfort. They clothed themselves in rags; they boasted that they never washed and lived in filth; it was a matter of pride to be covered by lice, to have wounds crawling with maggots and beds infested with bugs. One monk in the Egyptian desert made baskets out of reeds; for years he never changed the water in which the reeds were kept until the stench was unbearable. They ate only enough to keep themselves from death; they tortured themselves by not allowing themselves to sleep. They did everything possible to do away with anything that could bring joy into life. Centuries later Pascal used to wear a sharp-pointed belt next to his skin. If he ever felt happy he pressed the sharp points into his body so that the happiness might be banished by a feeling of pain.

Even as late as the nineteenth century, a distinguished theologian laid down that Jesus must have been a grave, serious child and a man who seldom smiled and never laughed. These things are obviously untrue. Jesus could not have been a gloomy person or children would not have loved him; and tax collectors and sinners would have been repelled, instead of being attracted. He could use illustrations which must have been given with a smile and which certainly must have raised a smile. He talked of a man with a plank in his own eye trying to remove a speck of dust from someone else's (Matthew 7:3,4). He talked of a camel, the most ungainly of beasts, trying to creep through a postern gate nick-named the needle's eye (Mark 10:25). (It may be that this is a picture of someone trying to thread a needle with a ship's hawser. *Kemelos* is Greek for a camel; and *kamilos* for a hawser, and in the time of Jesus they would be pronounced in exactly the same way.) The early Christians were described as *hilares*, the Latin adjective from which the English word 'hilarious' comes. There was about them what someone has called 'a certain holy hilarity.'

We do well to remember that Jesus likened the Kingdom to a feast. In its essence Christianity is a thing of joy. An unhappy Christian is a contradiction in terms. A great philosopher called laughter 'a sudden glory', as if when we laughed in sheer happiness we caught a glimpse of God himself. One of her students said of American college president Alice Freeman Palmer, 'she made me feel as if I were bathed in sunshine.'

The New Guests of God

The parable has a definitely local significance. The originally invited guests are the Jews. They were the chosen people. Their history was moulded to enable them to recognise and accept God's Son when he came into the world. In point of fact they refused the invitation and therefore others entered into the places reserved for them.

We must note an interesting touch in Luke's version of the parable. After the original guests had refused the invitation, the lame and maimed and blind are brought in. They stand for the *sinners* who, contrary to all their expectations, found in Jesus a welcoming friend.

But after they have come, in the servant reports, 'Still there is room', and yet more unexpected and unexpecting guests are gathered in from the highways and the hedges. These stand for the *Gentiles* to whom the Kingdom has been amazingly opened (Luke 14:21-23).

The original invitation of God, which had offered to the Jews the greatest privilege and the greatest responsibility, had been refused: now the door is wide open to the Gentiles whom the Jews had utterly despised. In the description of the Heavenly City in the book of the Revelation there is a suggestive passage. In Revelation 21:16 the dimensions of the city are given. It is a square, each wall of which measures 12,000 furlongs. A city whose walls measure 12,000 furlongs has an area of 2,250,000 *square miles.* That is to say, the City of God is so vast that there is room for every one from every nation.

We may note in the passing the harm that a too literalistic interpretation of scripture can do. The final command of the master to the slave in Luke 14:23 is, 'Go out ... and *compel* people to come in.' That word *compel* has been sadly misunderstood and misused. In the days of the Spanish Inquisition, when people were tortured to make them worship God in one particular way, it was used as justification. Of course we must do all we can to bring a fellow guest to the banquet of God, but the appeal must always be the appeal of love and never of grim constraint.

Excuses

The parable tells us that the invited guests '*all alike began to make excuses*' (Luke 14:18). The excuses are significant.

(1) The first said, 'I have bought a field and I must go out and see it' (Luke 14:18). That is the excuse of the man to whom business comes first. It is possible to become so obsessed with the activities of the world that the thought of the unseen things gets crowded out altogether and no time is left for prayer, worship and devotion. That is precisely the value of Sunday. If it were not for Sunday and for the call to worship, how often would we think of God at all? Sunday is a summons to think of things other than earthly activities. To abolish it, or to use it in purely secular ways, is a sure way to arrive in the end at a life

which has forgotten God. And the trouble about such a life is that it is a *life out of proportion.* Man is body, mind and spirit; or, if we like to put it more simply, body and soul. If he thinks so much of the material things that he forgets that he has a soul, he is bound to live an ill-proportioned life in which he is missing something. We must see to it that amidst the claims of business the claims of God are not forgotten.

(2) The second man said, 'I have bought five yoke of oxen, and I go to examine them' (Luke 14:19). That is the excuse of the man whose passion is novelty. He has a new possession and for the moment he is obsessed with it. Long ago Luke said of the Athenians that their one desire in life was either to tell or to hear something new (Acts 17:21). There are people whose danger is that when they encounter something new it drives everything else out of their minds. For a while, for instance, they may come to Church and worship with fidelity; then some new activity comes into life, some new friendship emerges, some new possession takes up their attention, and the claims of worship are abandoned for the something new. We must remember this—new things have their attraction and it is necessary to retain the adventurous mind which is not afraid of what is new, but at the same time certain things are *permanencies.* We may take a simple analogy from food. Unusual things are very attractive, but the body has certain basic needs which can be satisfied only by certain basic foods which are, as it were, the very staff of life; and, even amidst the novelties, the old and permanent things are necessary. Man's basic need is for God and therefore we must see to it that the call to worship and prayer is never passed over in the attraction of the new enthusiasms, the new activities, the new friendships which come into life.

(3) The third man said, 'I have married a wife, and therefore I cannot come' (Luke 14:20). This excuse outlines the demands of home. There is a paradox about our homes. They are the most important place in our lives; in one sense it is true to say that no claim can come above home. *But* it is possible to take an entirely selfish view of home. We can regard it as existing for nothing but our own convenience. We can make it a place where there is a world which no one but ourselves can enter.

We must remember two things. First, the great value of home is that it is a place into which a person may come in order to go out again refreshed for life. If it is a place which renders the person unfit for life, then it is failing in its function and it is being misused. We have a responsibility to the world as well as to our homes; our homes should not shut us off from the claims of God and of others, but should strengthen us better to discharge them.

Second, the New Testament insists that the Christian must be given to hospitality (Romans 12:13; 1 Peter 4:9). Homes are given to us not for our own selfish happiness, but that we may share our happiness with others, and specially with those who may not be so fortunate as ourselves.

The Insidious Excuses

One more thing—all the reasons the guests gave for not accepting the invitation were in themselves good reasons. It is right that a man should attend to his business, that he should be interested in what is new, that he should set the claims of home very high. One of the great dangers of life is that good things can come between us and Christ. If the tempting things always looked bad, we would seldom fall. The most insidious temptation of all is to let the good interfere with the best. We will be safe from that danger if we put first and foremost the claim of Jesus Christ.

23

Not having a Wedding Garment
Matthew 22:11-14

Rejected Guests

IN our Bible as it stands this reads as if it were the end of the Parable of the Wedding Feast; but it must originally have been a separate parable. It has been asked and with justice, 'How could the king condemn a man for not having a wedding garment when he had just been picked from the streets or the lanes, or the highways or the hedges, unexpectedly and with no chance of preparation?' Some have tried to get over this difficulty by saying that at such feasts wedding garments were actually provided for the guests to wear, but there is no evidence that there was any such custom. This is clearly a separate parable and it no doubt became attached to the other because it deals with something which happened at a wedding feast.

Here is a parallel story from Rabbi Jochanan ben Zakkai:

> It is like a king who invited his servants to a feast but he did not fix any time for the beginning of the feast. The wise ones among them arrayed themselves and sat at the entrance of the king's palace. They said, 'Something is still wanting in the king's palace, but we shall not have long to wait.' But the foolish ones among them went on with their ordinary work, saying, 'Is there ever a feast without long waiting?' Suddenly the king called for his servants. The wise ones among them entered in fitly arrayed, as they were. But the foolish ones entered into his presence all dirty as they were. Then did the king rejoice over the wise ones, but he was wrath with the foolish ones; and he said, 'These who arrayed themselves for the feast, let them recline and eat and drink; but these who did not array themselves for the feast, let them remain standing and watch the others.

The idea of guests who came unfittingly dressed and were condemned for doing so was familiar to the Jews.

A Warning to the Gentiles

The story Jesus told was of a man who came to a king's feast in his workday soiled clothes. The king asked him why. The man was speechless because he had no excuse; and for his discourtesy he was ejected from the feast.

In the first place this parable may well have had a local application in the mind of the early Church. It is suggestive that it is only Matthew who tells it. Matthew is the gospel which is specially interested in the Jews. Perhaps Matthew records this because he sees in it a warning to the Gentiles. True, the Gentiles are to be allowed in, but they must try to fit themselves for entry into the Kingdom of God.

It was always so easy to make a travesty of the gospel. The Jews had their laws and life became one long effort to keep them. Then Paul came and told men that it was not by keeping laws that they were saved, but by faith in the free grace of God. Now it was possible for a man to pervert the truth and say, 'All the laws are finished; I can do what I like and I can depend on the grace of God to forgive me.' There were actually those who argued like that. Paul dealt with them in Romans 6. They said, 'You say that the grace of God is wide enough to cover every sin? Well then, let us go on sinning to our hearts' content because, after all, the more we sin the more chance we give this wondrous grace of God to operate.' This was using Christian freedom as an excuse for un-Christian licence. It may well be, then, that Matthew is saying, 'It is true that there is a free invitation from God to the most unlikely people; but that does not absolve them from the duty of trying to fit themselves to be his guests.'

This duty was no longer a legal duty but a duty born of love. Let us take an analogy from life. If a person is to be presented at the royal court he must be dressed in a certain way. The law lays down that he will not get in unless he so arrays himself. That is a legal obligation. But suppose two people love each other. When they are meeting, they will come as attractively dressed as possible. That is no legal obligation; no law prescribes it; but because they love each other they feel bound to be at their best. So then it may be that Matthew is saying, 'Yes, you are released from all these laws; but surely the higher law of love will make you want to fit yourself to deserve the undeserved love of God.'

The Preparation for the Presence

In the parable however, there are lessons which are not local, but which last forever. The man without the garment was guilty of three faults.

(1) He had *no sense of the fitness of things*, otherwise he would not have turned up at a royal feast unkempt.

Edward Seago, the artist, tells how once he travelled with the gypsies painting pictures of them. In one town he took two little gipsy boys into a great cathedral. On the way they chattered and laughed; but once in the cathedral, without being told, they were as quiet as could be. The atmosphere of this place told them instinctively what was fitting; and instinctively we know what is the right kind of conduct for the presence of God.

But what we forget is this—we are apt to connect the presence of God with churches and cathedrals and to forget that the whole earth is his temple and that everywhere we are in his presence. It is not only in churches, but in all the world, that life must be fit for God to see. It was said of a great and good Greek, 'He moved through life as if he were ever living in the temple of the gods.' That does not abolish laughter and joy, for God loves these things; but it does abolish the mean things which are not fit for God to see.

(2) He had *no real sense of what was going on.* He must have come in with one idea—he wanted a meal. He had no thought of joining in the tribute to the king of which the feast was a part. It is almost impossible to share an occasion in any real sense if we do not know what is going on.

That means, for instance, that we must learn what worship really means. If we go to a symphony concert we enjoy it very much better if we know something about the instruments of the orchestra, about the structure of a symphony, about how the conductor conducts.

Sometimes if we know nothing about these things, the whole affair will be only a noise; but when we do know, the noise becomes intelligible. When we go to a church service we should try to have a clear idea of what is going on in every part of it, for only then can we really share in it.

(3) The man without the garment had *no reverence*. In other words, he had no respect for the king. We might define *reverence* as an awareness of the greatness of the person in whose presence we are. When we come to worship we are in the presence of God. We show whether or not we are aware of that in the smallest things. People often laugh at those who wear what are called Sunday clothes. It is true that no one should be kept out of, or stay away from, church because of a lack of good clothes to wear; but, at the same time, to do the best with what we have is an indication that we realise we are coming into the presence of the King. People will stand at attention when the National Anthem is played, but will slouch through the singing of a hymn; and yet the hymn is sung to the King of kings who is present at the service. *Reverence* means being aware into whose presence we are coming, and making our conduct, as far as we can, fit that presence.

Self-preparation

One general lesson this parable teaches—the necessity of preparing ourselves to come into the presence of God. Too often we leave home at the last moment, rush down the road and arrive without any preparation at all in the house of God. It would be well if for a moment or two before we came, we asked God to prepare us to enter into his presence.

24

Whatever is Right I will give You
Matthew 19:27-30; 20:1-16

Master and Workmen

IN many ways this is a puzzling parable, but when we set it against its background it will have lessons which are plain for all to see.

The hired servant was always engaged by the day and paid at the day's ending. 'The wages of a hired servant shall not remain with you all night until the morning' (Leviticus 19:13). 'You shall give him his hire on the day he earns it, before the sun goes down (for he is poor, and sets his heart upon it); lest he cry against you to the Lord, and it be sin in you' (Deuteronomy 24:15). Hired servants lived on the edge of destitution and this kindly provision of the law safeguarded their rights.

The Grape Harvest

There were certain times in Palestine when this story could actually have happened, especially at the grape harvest which came at the end of August and the early part of September. By the middle of September the rains came and it was always a race with the weather to get the crop in. At such a time every available man would be pressed into service. The Jewish day ran from 6 am to 6 pm The hours when the men were engaged were therefore 6 am, 9 am, 12 midday, 3 pm, and finally 5 pm. At the time of the harvest, with the rains threatening to come, it was quite possible that the owner of a vineyard would employ men even as late as 5 o'clock in the evening. The denarius was the normal day's wage for a working man. But the amazing thing is that no matter how long a man had worked, he got the same pay; those who had only worked from 5 o'clock in the evening got exactly the same as those who had worked the long twelve hours from 6 in the morning.

Quality not Quantity

All kinds of meanings have been extracted from this parable. It has been suggested that it is the quality and not the quantity of a man's work that counts. That is true, though there is no suggestion in the parable that the last to be engaged were any better workers than the first.

The importance of quality was a common lesson of the Rabbis. Here is a Rabbinic parable along these lines:

> It is like a king who hired many labourers, and there was one labourer who understood his work beyond measure well. What did the king do? He caused him to accompany him as he strolled along many pathways. When evening was come those labourers drew near to receive their wage and he gave each the full amount of his wage. But the labourers murmured and said, 'We have toiled the whole day, and this man has toiled but two hours, and yet he has given him the same wages as we have received.' Then spake the king to them, 'He has done more work in two hours than you have during the whole day.'

There is indeed a lesson here. A comparatively small piece of work done with care and diligence may be of more value than a greater amount of work done in the most slapdash way. We do not judge an author's greatness by the amount of literature that he produces, but by its quality. Many who wrote one priceless gem of a poem are remembered; while many who wrote many volumes are forgotten, because their work was second-rate.

Jews and Gentiles

It is possible that the parable carries a rebuke for the Jews. Always they regarded themselves as the chosen people of God and therefore entitled to special privileges. For all their national history they had been God's people. Not unnaturally they would resent that all the privileges of God were now open to the Gentiles. How could they be entitled to the same as the Jews?

They were wrong because they looked on God in the wrong way. They regarded God as a Judge, a Task-master, a Law-giver. If God were only that, then he would, with a scrupulous balance, give to men precisely what they had earned. But God is Father. A father does not love his eldest son more that his youngest, even if the eldest in twenty years older. Love does not nicely calculate the more or less. All members of the human family are loved equally just because they are sons and daughters. And all members of God's family are equally dear to God.

Soon or Late

That could be widened farther. It might be held that the parable declares that those who come to God at the beginning of their lives are not loved more than those who come at the end. It may be that a person becomes a Christian in his earliest days; or it may be that he does not become a Christian until the evening shadows are falling on his life. In Revelation 21:13 we are told that on every side of the Holy City there are three gates. It might well be that the gates on the east are for those who come into the friendship of God in the morning of their days; and the ages on the west are for those who come in the time of the westering sun. But to God it makes no difference. There are no distinctions in the love of God.

The Right to Work

Some scholars have seen in this parable two great economic truths. The first is the right of every man to a day's work. One passage has great pathos. It was the custom for workmen to come and stand in the village square until someone hired them. See what happens. At 5 o'clock in the evening the master came; men were still standing there, waiting with the forlorn hope that someone might yet give them work to do. If not, they would have to go home to the bitterness of a hungry family. The master asked, 'Why are you standing here doing nothing?' There is infinite pathos in the answer—'No one will give us any work to do.'

We may sometimes think it would be splendid to do nothing all the time. But unemployment is a terrible thing. Hugh Martin tells us that his old teacher, the classical scholar Sir Henry Jones, used to say that the most tragic words in all Shakespeare were 'Othello's occupation's gone.'

It must always be remembered that for the larger part of his life Jesus was a working man. Until he was thirty years of age he was the village carpenter of Nazareth. He knew all the difficulties of making a living and of supporting a mother and younger brothers and sister. It may well be that this is why he worked some of his miracles. Luke (6:6-10) tells us of the healing of the man with the paralysed hand on the Sabbath, in defiance of the watching Scribes and Pharisees. With a curious touch Luke tells us that it was the man's *right* hand. Tradition has it that the man was a stonemason and that his paralysis had taken his work away. Here is a poem which embodies the man's joy at getting his hand and his work back again.

Praise God! Praise God! Give me my tools again!
Oh, let me grasp a hammer and a saw;
Bring me a nail and any piece of wood;
Come see me shut my hand and open it,
And watch my nimble fingers twirl a ring.
How good are solids—oak and stone and iron.
And rough and smooth and straight and curved and round.

Here Rachel: for these long and weary years
My hand has ached to smooth your shining hair
And touch your dimpled cheek; come, wife, and see
I am a man again, a man for work,
A man for earning bread and clothes and home,
A man and not a useless hold-the-hand,
A man, no more a bandaged cumberer.

And did you hear them muttering at Him,
And did you see them looking sour at me?
They'll cast me from the synagogue perchance,

144

But let them: I've a hand, a hand, a hand.
And, ah dear wife, to think He goes about
So quietly and does such things as this
Making poor half men whole ....

(Anon)

There we catch the joy of the man who can work again. In a really Christian civilisation no one's skill would waste in idleness; our right of to a day's work would be recognised.

A Living Wage

Further, it has been suggested that this parable lays down the right of every one to a living wage. The master might have cut the pay of the late-comers, but he knew well, that were he to do so, there would be hungry homes that night and on the morrow. Therefore, recognising the right of the late-comers to a living wage, he paid them in full.

Jesus was intensely concerned with material things. He was not so heavenly-minded that he forgot about the practical needs and problems of this life. He had worked himself and he knew that men must eat to live. He fed their hungry bodies as he fed their souls. In a truly Christian society no one could bear that others had too little while they had too much.

The Spirit of Work

But the real lesson of this parable is that it is the spirit in which work is done which makes all the difference. Let us look at its context. It comes immediately after Peter said to Jesus, 'Master, we have left everything and followed you,' and then quite bluntly added, 'What do we get out of it?' Now let us return to the parable. It is stressed that the first-comers came to an agreement with the master (Matthew 20:2,13). Maybe they haggled. Certainly their spirit was, 'We work if you give us so much pay.' In the case of the late-comers there was no agreement. In fact verse 4 rules out an agreement. The master was

145

to pay as he liked. The late-comers made no protest: their attitude was, 'Pay me what you like, but give me a job to do.'

It is easy in any sphere of life—shop, restaurant, factory or office —to recognise the person who has no idea of serving the public but is simply doing the irreducible minimum to ensure a wage.

There is a famous story of Thomas Carlyle's father. In the church in which he was an elder, a dispute broke out with the minister about a matter of salary. After the wrangle had gone on some time, Carlyle's father rose and spoke one sentence, 'Give the hireling his wages and let him go.' It is easy in every sphere to recognise the person who is a hireling and it is easy to salute the great souls who are not.

One of the most famous of modern poets was A E Housman, author of 'A Shropshire Lad.' He stipulated that he should receive no royalties, but that any profits should be used to issue cheaper editions; he returned cheques sent to him from the sale of American editions. He said he had written it because he could not help himself. 'I would no more think,' he said, 'of selling what has been wrung from my heart than of cutting off my right hand and sending it to the market place.'

There are two real motives for work. One is service of our fellow men. Take, for instance, a girl who works in a hospital as a radiographer. For all practical purposes it will suffice if the hospital patients are numbers on a card index. But she knows it will help them if she can remember their names; and so she makes the effort to turn the numbers into names and the index cards into people. She is working not for pay but to serve others. Service of others, not profit for self, must be the Christian principle.

The other motive is service of God. Jenny Lind, a famous singer known as the 'Swedish nightingale' was a devoted Christian. A few moments before she was due to go on to the platform for any concert, she shut everyone else out of her dressing-room. Then she would stand and very softly sing a note in her magnificent voice; and then she would pray, 'Christ, let me sing true tonight.' She was singing for God.

George Eliot in her poem on Antonio Stradivari, the maker of the famous Stradivarius violins, describes how Antonio felt that while

God gave the great musicians music, he gave them the violins to play. Then comes the thought to him:

If my hand slacked
I should rob God ...
He could not make
Antonio Stradivari's violins
Without Antonio.

He was working for God.

Any one can do that. God wants people to be happy and healthy. It is then clear that the doctor, nurse, surgeon and radiographer are working for God. But if people are to be well, they must be fed and clothed: therefore the farmer, baker, tailor and shoemaker, are all working for God. If these products are to be of any use, they must be sold and delivered: therefore the person at the counter, in the office, on the railway, on the road, the boy delivering the messages, are all working for God. Any task which is useful to the world is done for God. When we see it that way, a new thrill will enter into work: we will work not for pay, but for men and for God; and the reward we get in the end will be beyond price.

25

Well done!

Matthew 25:14-30

The Entrusted Money

A TALENT was a very large sum of money. The word does not really mean a coin at all. It signifies a weight. Jesus told of a master who intended to be abroad for some considerable time. Not wishing his estate to lie idle during his long absence, he divided it among his servants in proportion to their ability. To one he gave five talents, to another two, and to another one. After a long time he came home again and summoned the servants to a reckoning. The first two had actually doubled the money entrusted to them. But the third, making the excuse that he had been afraid to risk his talent by trading with it, had simply hidden the money in the ground, and now he handed it back with no increase. The first two were praised and given promise of greater things to come; the third man was condemned and shut out in the outer darkness.

The Condemnation of the Orthodox

This parable had undoubtedly a local significance in the first place. It has been pointed out by C H Dodd that the whole attention is concentrated on the unworthy servant. Who then does he stand for? Undoubtedly, he stands for the Scribes and the Pharisees and the orthodox Jews. Their one aim in life was to keep things as they were. They said themselves that all that they wanted was to build a fence round the law. That is why they crucified Jesus. He came with new ideas about God, about life and about a man's duty in life; and because they would have nothing to do with new ideas they crucified him.

Here surely is a challenge to adventurous religion. In the Christian faith there must be steady development. God is infinite; no man can ever get to the end of God. The riches of Christ are unsearchable; no man can exhaust them. And therefore every generation should be penetrating deeper and deeper into the truth of God. Every man all his life should be learning more and more about God.

Yet the whole tendency in orthodox religion is exactly the other way. It is so easy to worship the past, to look back on what we believe to have been a golden age, instead of forward to the greater things which shall be. Bishop Lesslie Newbigin tells how, when plans for the united Church in South India were being discussed, one of the things that kept holding matters up was the demand to know where this course of action was leading. When this had gone on for some time, someone rose and said, 'The demand to know where we are going is one which no Christian has a right to make.' The Christian must follow truth as blind men long for light, wherever that truth may lead.

Dr Fosdick, in one of his books, draws this analogy: what would happen to medicine if doctors were not allowed to take cognisance of any discovery made later than the seventeenth century? In the life of the Church, there is something far wrong if in almost three hundred years men have not learned more about the meaning of their religion. In the individual life there is something wrong if a person's faith remains exactly the same at twenty as it was at ten, or at forty as it was at twenty. This parable is a challenge to be adventurous enough to follow our thought and the guidance of the Holy Spirit wherever they may lead.

To Him that hath

To this parable another saying became attached which gave it a wider meaning. In Matthew the parable nears the end with the saying that the man who already has will receive still more, while the man who has not will lose what he has. It is interesting to note that Mark (4:25) gives that saying in quite a different context; but it comes in very aptly as Matthew gives it at the conclusion of this parable. To the Jews it was a common idea. Rabbi Johanan said, 'God gives wisdom only to him who possesses wisdom.' Hillel, one of the greatest doctors of Jewish law, said, 'He who increases not, decreases.'

This is a universal law of life. The more knowledge we have, the more we are able to receive. The pupil who knows only a little Latin cannot know the lovely things in Latin literature. But the more he knows, the more he can appreciate the wealth of the classics. The person who knows only a little about science cannot understand the vast things of scientific knowledge; but the more he learns, the greater the wonders he is capable of understanding. The reverse is equally true. If we have a little knowledge and make no attempt to develop it, we end by losing what we have. Suppose a girl learns to play the piano a little; and then suppose she never opens it, never practises; ultimately she will forget altogether how to play it. Many have learned a smattering of French at school but afterwards never use it and forget even the little that they learned. Here we are face to face with a great and important truth—in life we can never stand still; if we are not going forward, we must go backward. We must then see to it that every day we advance, know something new, do something a little better.

Differing Gifts

Even when we have taken these lessons out of this parable, there remains much richness in it. One thing stands out. The servants were given differing amounts. Each was given an amount to suit his ability. It was not demanded that they should do what they could not do. Jesus never held that all men were equal in ability.

We are all born with different abilities and the test is how we use the abilities we have. It therefore becomes clear that the whole duty of life is not to envy someone else their skill, but to make the best of our own. It was a favourite saying of Foch, the great soldier, that the art of warfare consists in doing the best one can with the resources one has. Life is like that. But though we cannot be equal in achievement, we can be equal in effort. The ultimate aim in life must be to say in all sincerity, 'I have done my best.'

The Man who would not try

Further, this parable condemns the man who would not try. The unworthy servant never tried. It is one of the greatest of all sins to come to a state when we do not care, when we do not want to try.

Very likely the unworthy servant felt that it was not worth trying. He had only one talent and it did not seem worth while trying to use it. But the world is not composed of geniuses. For the most part it is composed of ordinary people doing ordinary jobs, but these ordinary jobs must be done if the world is to go on and God's plans worked out. It has been said with great wisdom, 'God does not want extraordinary people who do extraordinary things nearly so much as he wants ordinary people who do ordinary things extraordinarily well.' Abraham Lincoln once said, 'God must love the common people because he made so many of them.' The world depends on the man with the one talent.

To lose or to use

Again, this parable lays down that what we do not use we are bound in the end to lose. It is not long before life teaches us that. We may have certain skills and abilities; but if we do not use them we soon lose them. It is so with games; if we do not practise we lose such ability as we have. It is so with knowledge; if we do not keep our knowledge polished we lose it. It is so with even greater things. In the autobiography of Charles Darwin there is a famous and pathetic passage. He tells how, when he was young, he used to find delight in poetry and music. As he became older he grew so immersed in the study of biology that he gave absolutely no time to reading poetry or listening to music. So, he tells us, he came to a stage when poetry meant nothing to him and music only a meaningless noise; and he went on to say that if he had his life to live over again, he would see to it that some time was given to these things so that they would not be lost. If we honestly examine our lives we will see that there is some talent which God has given us. It is death to hide that talent; it is life to use it in the service of men and God.

F

26

Faithful in Little
Luke 19:11-27

A Matter of History

THERE is a close resemblance between this parable and the parable of the talents. Perhaps they are two versions of the same story, or perhaps Jesus used the same story in slightly different forms on two different occasions.

There is one very interesting thing about this version. We have seen that Jesus in his parables frequently takes incidents from everyday life to illustrate the great truths. He desires to teach. But it may well be that here he uses for the one and only time an incident from history. The parable tells of a king who went to claim a kingdom, whose subjects sent an embassy of protest, who was given the kingdom and who took a stern revenge on his opponents. In the year 4 BC Herod the Great died; he had the title of king but always subject to the permission and the good will of Rome. It had been expected that he would will his kingdom to his son Antipas; but he altered his will and left it instead to his son Archelaus. Before Archelaus could inherit he had to go to Rome to receive permission to do so. The Jews promptly sent an embassy of fifty men to Rome to beg that the kingdom not be given to him. Augustus the Roman Emperor heard the embassy but gave Archelaus the kingdom. He did not, however, allow him the title of kings until he had proved himself worthy of it, which in fact he never did. These are exactly the circumstances in the parable and it looks as if for once Jesus is taking an incident from history to teach his lesson.

As we can

This parable repeats many of the lessons of the parable of the talents; but there are others we may add. The nobleman did not demand the same result from every man. It was true that all received the same amount this time. For all that an equal achievement was not demanded from each of them. The one who had turned his £1 into £10 and the other who had turned he £1 into £5 were both praised.

God does not demand the same from everyone. He knows well that people have different abilities. God's demand is not 'How great is your work?', not even 'How good is your work?', but 'Is this the best you can do?' In school, and usually in the world, it is the highest mark which receives the highest prize. But even in school it may well be that a 55 per cent mark from a scholar who is not very clever, represents more honest toil than a 90 per cent from a scholar who finds things easy. God knows about these things and God sets the right value on our efforts when we do our best.

The Little Job first

This parable teaches, too, that if we would some day be given a great task we must first prove ourselves by doing the little jobs well. It was because they had been faithful in quite small things that the servants were given greater tasks to do.

Black American Booker Washington was one of the greatest men in the world. By the end of his life he was Principal of Tuskegee University and held in honour by all. But when he was young it was very difficult for a black boy to obtain a college education at all. Undeterred, he heard of a university where he would be accepted as a student and he tramped for miles to get there. But there were no places left. They offered him a job sweeping the floors and making the beds in the dormitories. He took it at once, and did that menial job so well that soon he was admitted as a student.

It is impossible to start at the top and it would be bad for us if we could. It is foolish to despise the small jobs and to think they do not matter. It is by doing the lesser thing well that we prove ourselves fit for the bigger thing.

More Work to do

Further, this parable illustrates a great truth; the reward of work well done is more work to do. The servants who had done so well were not told to sit back and rest; they were given still more responsibility and still greater tasks to do. In many spheres we accept that principle. The actor who is playing a small part longs for the day when he will be given a bigger role. The surgeon beginning his career longs for the day when the hardest operations will be delegated to him.

We should always remember that it is not an infliction but a compliment to be given a task to do. The general chooses his best soldiers for his hardest tasks. The teacher puts his best students in for the hardest examinations. The trainer makes his best players and athletes training the hardest. The bigger the task and the more often the tasks are given to us, the bigger the compliment which is being paid to us. The higher we rise in the world's work, the heavier the responsibilities. The real man regards a task not as something to be avoided, but as a challenge to prove himself and as a compliment to his ability.

The King's Return

Both parables speak of the day when the master came back and demanded account. In the early days people believed that Jesus was going to come back to this world at any moment. They expected him soon, certainly within their own lifetime. That did not happen. It is useless to speculate when it will happen; but the day *will* come when we will be called to account for the way in which we have used this life and the talents which God gave to us. It will make us work far better if we remember that all our work must some day pass the test of God. George Eliot wrote of Antonio Stradivari that he winced at all false work and loved the true. At all our work we must remember that we must do it in such a way that it is fit for God to see.

27

Joy in Heaven
Luke 15:1-7

The Good Shepherd

AS we study this Parable of the Lost Sheep, we should have before us Jesus' picture of himself as the Good Shepherd (John 10:1-18). In Palestine the shepherd was a familiar figure. In view of that, it is interesting to note that in the strict sections of the Jews the shepherd was despised. In the very nature of his calling he could not observe the petty rules and regulations; he could not always observe the hours of prayer; he could not perform all the minute regulations of hand-washing before he ate; the claims of his flock made such things impossible and the result was that those who thought themselves good looked down on the shepherd as being low in the scale of religious precedence.

The Shepherd's Equipment

There were certain things which every shepherd possessed and used. He had his *rod and staff.* The rod was like a shepherd's crook. He used it for walking and for catching any sheep which was straying away. At night, when the flock was going into the fold, the shepherd held his rod across the gateway, just slightly above the ground. Every sheep had to pass under the rod as it entered the fold. As it did so the shepherd quickly looked at it to see if it had been injured during the day or if it was sickly. So God says in Ezekiel (20:37) speaking to the people of Israel, 'I will make you pass under the rod.' Just as the shepherd cared for the sheep, so God cares for his people. The staff was the shepherd's weapon. It was a stout stick three or four feet long, with a ball of wood about the size of an orange on top of it. The shepherd used it as a weapon to combat marauders and to drive off wild beasts.

In addition to these, the shepherd had his *water-skin*; his *scrip* where carried the food he needed; and, most important of all, his *sling*. Shepherds were experts with the sling and could, as the Old Testament says, sling to a hair's breadth. There was one rather curious use of the sling. There were no sheep-dogs and the shepherd often used the sling to do the work a sheep-dog might do. If a sheep were straying away, the shepherd would drop a stone immediately in front of it with his sling, and turn it back. For his dress the shepherd wore a sheep-skin robe, usually with the fleece turned inwards for warmth.

The Shepherd and the Sheep

In Palestine the relationship between sheep and shepherd was much closer than in our country. Sheep in Palestine were rarely kept for killing, but for their wool; and therefore a sheep was often in the flock for anything up to eight or nine years. The shepherd called the sheep by name (John 10:3), and did not walk behind them as in this country, but in front (John 10:4). Thus when the flock came to any narrow rocky defile where robbers of wild beasts might lurk, the shepherd was first to meet the danger. He risked his life to save his sheep.

Each shepherd had a peculiar call which his flock recognised. They would answer the call of their own shepherd and not of any other (John 10:3 and 5). The travel writer H V Morton tells how he saw two flocks of sheep being put together into a communal fold in Bethlehem. He wondered how they would ever be sorted out when morning came, but it was very simple. The shepherds stood one on either side of the entry to the fold and each gave his own peculiar cry; and each sheep ran to its own shepherd. In the fold there was no door, only an open space by which the sheep went in and out. At night the shepherd lay across that open space so that no sheep could get out and no raider could get in, except over his body. He was literally the door (John 10:9).

The Village Shepherds

Even the towns and the villages would know all about shepherds. In them were communal flocks and shepherds. The sheep were collected in the morning and brought back at night. The shepherd was held to be absolutely responsible for what happened to the sheep. If a sheep was ill he must tend it: and often the shepherd might have been seen tramping home with a sheep on his shoulders or a lamb in the bosom of his sheep-skin robe. If a sheep died, the shepherd was bound to produce its fleece to show how it had died. If a sheep was lost, the shepherd must seek until he found it. The shepherds were experts in tracking sheep from their hoof-prints and often would trace a sheep for miles. When the communal flocks came home, the people of the village might note that there was one shepherd missing; they would know that somewhere out in the wilds he was searching for a sheep that was lost; they would watch and when at last he came in sight with the sheep which had been lost, there would indeed be great rejoicing that the sheep was found. There is one other point which is of interest. In the parable the shepherd leaves the 99 sheep and goes off to find one. When we think of it, that seems the surest way of losing the 99 as well; but we must think of a group of communal shepherds. The sheep were left in their charge while the shepherd went to look for the sheep that had strayed away.

UNTIL SHE FIND IT (LUKE 15:8-10)

The Coin that was lost

Here is a picture taken from everyday home life. Maybe Jesus had seen it happen in his own home. The coin in question was a *drachma*, a silver coin worth about a shilling. It may have been one of two things. It may simply have been part of the slender resources of that household. We must remember that in Palestine in the time of Jesus a working man's day's wage was almost a shilling; and to lose a drachma would be financial disaster. But perhaps it is more likely that the ten silver pieces had to do with a Jewish marriage custom. Every Jewish girl scraped and saved until she had ten silver pieces which were then strung together and worn as a necklace or a head-dress. It was her own property and remained absolutely so; it could not be taken even for debt. Without it she could not be married, for it was the sign of a married woman. It was the nearest ancient equivalent to a marriage ring. If the lost coin was one of those ten, it had a sentimental value even greater than its purchasing power.

We are given a vivid picture of the search. First the little oil lamp is lit. The humbler Palestinian houses were very dark for they were lit by a circular window only 18 inches (45 centimetres) or so across. The broom was made of palm leaves. The search was difficult because there was no proper flooring, only the tramped down earth covered with dried reeds and rushes. It was not to clean the house the woman swept on this occasion. It was to dislodge the coin from its hiding-place so that she would hear the tinkle, or catch the glint when it moved amongst the rushes. As we read this story we are at home in a village house in Palestine.

HE WAS LOST AND IS FOUND (LUKE 15:11-32)

The Father and his Sons

Under Jewish law a father could not leave his property to whoever he wished. He was bound to leave two-thirds to the elder son and one-third to the younger (Deuteronomy 21:17). It was not uncommon for a father to divide his estate before he died. He might feel that he was past the claims of business, or that he wanted leisure in the evening of his years and he would hand over his property to his sons. For all that, the request of the younger son bears a certain callousness: in effect, he is saying, 'Father, when you are dead, I'll get this share anyway. Give it to me now.'

When he went off to the far country, the depths of degradation to which he sank can be seen from the employment in which he found himself. He was feeding swine, which were unclean animals (Leviticus 11:7) and with which no orthodox Jew could have anything to do. The husks were the carob nuts which were the food of animals and of the utterly destitute. When the son came home, he intended to make the request that his father should employ him as a hired servant. That was the lowest rank of all. In a large estate there were three kinds of servants. There were those generally called *bondmen.* In theory they were slaves, but in fact they were almost part of the family and they had certain definite rights which are laid down in Exodus 21:2-6 and Leviticus 25:39-47. There were *servants.* These were the subordinates of the bondmen. Their lives were harder, but again they were regarded as being on the circumference of the family. Lowest of all were the *hired servants.* They were hired by the day; at any moment and without warning or reason they might be dismissed; they often lived on the verge of complete destitution.

It was to the lowest rank of all that the son meant to beg admission. But one of the most significant things about the parable is that he never even got the chance to make his request (Luke 15:21). Before he had time to say all he meant to say, his father interrupted and gave orders for a very different kind of reception. In Luke 15:22 each of the three things the father mentions has its own significance. The *robe* stands for honour; it was the first or the best robe; it was not to disgrace but to honour that the son came home. The *ring* stands for mastery. The ring would be a signet ring; and when a master gave his ring to a servant or a father to his son, it meant that he was handing into his control all his possessions. The *shoes* stand for the status of son. Slaves went barefoot but the children of the family went shod.

The Gospel within the Gospels

Someone has called chapter 15 of St Luke 'the gospel within the gospels.' It is regarded as the very essence of the faith. Let us then see if we can penetrate the meaning of these parables. Above all they make clear *God's attitude to the sinner.* They arise from a situation in which Jesus was criticised for being friends with tax collectors and sinners. So these parables teach us first, that *God wants the sinner.* That is precisely what the strict Jew could not understand. They were quite certain that God approved of good people, but had no use whatsoever for the sinner. Three times Jesus talked about the joy that comes when something which has been lost is found. To the Jew this would come as a staggering shock, for they had a saying, 'There is joy before God when those who provoke him perish from the world.' Let us take some kind of remote analogy. When a doctor sees a sick person, the one thing he wants to do is to make that sick person well again, and he will go to any trouble to achieve that desire. It would be terrible if doctors felt that all sick people should be destroyed. The glory of the medical profession lies in the fact that it is its great task to make sick people well.

The Jews regarded God, we may put it, as a doctor who had no use for sick people and wished nothing but their elimination. Jesus regarded God as a doctor whose aim was to make well again all who were ill with the disease of sin. However bad men are, God still wants them. The Jew to some extent would have agreed with that—on one condition: if the sinner repented and came crawling back on his hands and knees, God might accept him. They had lovely sayings, 'Open thou for Me a gateway of penitence as big as a needle's eye and I will open for you gates wide enough for chariots and horses.' 'God's hand is stretched out under the wings of the heavenly chariot to snatch the penitent from the grasp of justice.' But note this—the first Jewish reaction is that God wants nothing to do with the sinner; the second and gentler is that God will accept the sinner if he comes beseeching to him. Now here is the second utterly new thing Jesus says in these parables: he says that *God goes out to seek the sinner* or that *he is actually waiting and watching for the sinner to come home.* The Jew might in his gentler moments agree that God would accept a penitent sinner; but he never dreamed of a God who went out to *look* for sinners. The shepherd searched for the sheep; the woman searched for the coin; God searches for men.

God the Father

Why should that be? There are two typical names for God. Although not absolutely so, it is broadly true that one belongs to the Old Testament and the other to the New. In the Old Testament God is typically *King*. A king desires the loyalty of his subjects; but, should his

160

subjects rebel against him, he will in the end be compelled to exercise force and either to obliterate them or to bring them to heel. In the New Testament, God is typically *Father*. However large his family, a father cannot spare one. Even if one turns against him and causes him infinite sorrow, the last thing he wants is the obliteration of that child; he wants him to come back. The difference between a king's affection for his people and a father's love for his children is that in the nature of things a king's love cannot be individualised. A father's always is. A king sees men in the mass but, as the old saint had it, 'God loves each one of us, as if there were only one of us to love.'

In one sense that is what we mean when we call the Christian God a person. Many thinkers have thought of God as The First Cause, or The Divine Energy, or The Life Force. These are not persons. The essence of a person is that he needs others. He can find happiness only in the love and fellowship and friendship of others. In all reverence we may say that it is so with God. James Weldon Johnson, wrote a strange poem called 'The Creation', in which he used ideas that a child might use:

And God stepped out on space
And he looked around and said:
I'm lonely—
I'll make me a world.

Then God walked around,
And God looked around
On all that he had made.
He looked at his sun,
And he looked at his moon,
And he looked at his little stars;
He looked on his world
With all its living things,
And God said: I'm lonely still.

Then God sat down—
On the side of a hill where he could think.

By a deep wide river he sat down;
With his head in his hands,
God thought and thought.
Till he thought: I'll make me a man!

In its strange way that poem tells us the truth. The God we believe in searches for men because he is a person and needs the love of other persons.

The Difference in the Parables

These three Parables—the Lost Sheep, the Lost Coin and the Lost Son —are very like each other, and yet each of them has its own particular impact. They do not simply say the same thing three times in slightly different ways. There are genuine differences.

(1) *The coin was lost because someone lost it.* That means there are people who fall into wrong ways through the fault of others. Someone tells of an old man who was dying. One thing worried him. When he was a boy, he and some other boys had been playing at a crossroads. The signpost there was loose in its socket and they turned it round so that its arms were facing in the wrong directions. The one thing that worried him now was the thought that someone might have been sent on the wrong road by what he had done. It is bad to sin, but it is still worse to teach another to sin.

(2) *The sheep was lost because of its foolishness.* We can go wrong because we will not think. One of the best rules before we embark on any action is to ask ourselves not how this looks at the present moment, but how it will look when time has passed. We would be saved from many mistakes if we stopped to think.

(3) *The son was lost because he quite deliberately took his own way.* There are those who know what is wrong and still do it. Most of us are in that category. We have the voice of conscience, the guidance of God's Book, the experience and advice of those who are older and wiser than we, the lessons which life teaches us, and yet we take the wrong way. We may note one thing. The father made no attempt to dissuade the son from going away. He did not argue with

him; he let him go. It may well be that he was thinking that his son had to learn the hard way. But surely it is far better to accept God's will in the first place than to be driven to accept it after we have found how painful the consequences of the wrong way can be.

The Elder Brother

In the Parable of the Prodigal Son there remains one character—the *elder brother*. It is sometimes felt that we deal too harshly with him. But the story is full of revealing touches. He stands for the Pharisees who were angry that God should have any use for tax collectors and sinners.

(1) In verse 29 he says, 'Lo, these many years I have served you.' All the time he had been working he had been grimly doing his duty. He had no thrill, no pride, no love in his work; it was a burdensome duty. When Stevenson lived in the South Sea Islands he had a native boy who always woke him in the morning with tea and toast. One day this boy was ill and another was taking his place. He woke Stevenson not only with the tea and toast, but with a beautifully cooked omelette as well. When Stevenson saw it, he said to him, 'Boy, great is your wisdom.' 'No, master,' said the boy, 'but great is my love.' It is service given in love, not in grim duty, that God wants.

(2) In verse 29 the elder brother says, 'I never disobeyed your command.' He was utterly self-righteous; he regarded himself as a good man without any faults. It has been said, and said truly, that the greatest fault is to be conscious of no fault. Self-righteousness shuts us off both from God and mankind.

(3) In verses 30 and 32 there is another revealing touch. The elder brother refers to the returned prodigal as 'this son of yours.' He will not call him brother. But the father speaks of 'this your brother,' compelling him to remember. The elder brother, because he was self-righteous, always had his eyes focused to find fault and a tongue tuned to criticise. He was the kind of man who would rather see someone punished than forgiven. His whole attitude is that of contempt. And the man who looks down on his fellow men can never know the fellowship of God.

(4) In essence the elder brother stands for the goodness which is unattractive. There are two words in Greek for *good*. One is *agathos* and means simply that a thing is good in quality. The other is *kalos* and means not only that a thing is good, but that it has a sheen and a winsomeness which makes it a lovely thing. Real Christian goodness is an attractive thing. Struthers of Greenock used to say that it would help the Church more than anything else if Christians sometimes did bonnie things. The elder brother was in a sense a good man; but his goodness was hard, and unlovely, because he had none of the father's love in his heart.

The Loving Father

We note one thing more. For centuries the third parable has been called the Parable of the Prodigal Son. It would be far better if we were to call it the Parable of the Loving Father, for it is the father and not the son who is the hero of the story.

28

Go in Peace
Luke 7:36-50

The Scene and the Characters

IN this most lovely story let us look first at the scene. Jesus sat at a meal in the house of Simon the Pharisee. We have seen in our previous studies that the houses of the poor were very small and consisted of one room. The houses of the wealthy consisted of a series of rooms opening on to an open air courtyard, where there might be a garden and a pool. In the warm weather meals were eaten in the courtyard. The table was a low block-like structure. People in those days did not sit on chairs to eat. They used low couches. They might do so in one of two ways. Either they knelt at the table with the feet stretched out behind; or, more usually, they reclined, leaning on the left elbow with the right hand free, and again the feet stretched out behind.

Rabbis led a very public life. When they were walking along the roads they were followed by crowds eager to hear even their passing words; and even when they were dining, people came to stand behind them and listen to the wise things they had to say. There is then nothing surprising in the fact that the woman in the parable had penetrated into the courtyard of Simon's house. She would be only one of many who had come to catch the pearls of wisdom which fell from the wise teacher's lips.

Now we come to the characters in the story. Simon was a Pharisee. Remember that the name *Pharisee* means 'the separated one.' The Pharisees were men whose whole lives were dedicated to the keeping of the slightest regulation of the law and who looked with contempt on those who were not as meticulous as themselves. It may seem strange to find a Pharisee inviting Jesus to a meal in his house. There are three possible reasons why he may have done so.

(1) He may really have felt that Jesus had something to say. In verse

40 he addresses him as *Teacher* or *Rabbi,* giving Jesus the technical address of respect.

(2) It has been suggested that Simon's orthodox friends had delegated to him the duty of inviting Jesus to a meal with a view to examining every word Jesus said, so that a charge of heresy and blasphemy could perhaps be framed against him.

(3) Perhaps the most likely reason is that Simon was what someone has called a collector of celebrities. He invited Jesus to his table as a kind of interesting specimen. The fact that he gave to Jesus none of the usual courtesies rather supports this view. He was treating Jesus with the half-amused, half-contemptuous interest that is given to an odd specimen of humanity whom a superior person wishes to examine at closer quarters.

The woman was a notorious character. Even if she had not been so, it would have been shocking for a Jewish teacher to be seen speaking to a woman in public; and because she was a woman of such reputation, Jesus' action was doubly astounding to those who were watching him.

The Action of the Story

Something about Jesus had gone straight to the woman's heart. Maybe she had heard of him as the friend of sinners like herself and had listened to him speak; and now she could not tear herself away from his presence. Then all her love ran over. She began to weep and her tears fell on Jesus' feet. For a woman to unbind her hair in public was considered in those days the height of immodesty; in fact the Jews considered unbound hair the trademark of a harlot. But such was this woman's love that she had lost all self-consciousness; she no longer cared what people thought of her; and she wiped the tears from his feet with her long hair. Round her neck she wore a little phial of perfume as most Jewish women did. Sometimes these phials were very valuable. Pure balsam was worth its weight in silver, and spikenard too was very valuable. It was the most precious thing she possessed; and she broke it and poured it over Jesus' feet. And such was her love that she kept kissing his feet.

All this time Simon had been shocked at what was going on. He kept thinking that Jesus could not be a prophet or he would have known what kind of woman this was and would not have allowed her near him. The last thing on earth that Simon would have allowed would have been to let this woman touch him. As Augustine said long ago, 'Jesus heard Simon thinking.' So Jesus said to him, 'Simon, I have something to say to you.'

There were certain customs of hospitality which it was grave discourtesy to omit. The roads in Palestine were not surfaced. In the hot weather they were inches deep in dust, and in the wet they were rivers of mud. Sandals were merely leather soles held in place by a strap and giving little protection to the feet. So when a guest arrived, there was invariably a servant at the door with a great jar of cool, clean water, to cleanse the guest's feet. When the guest went to the table, a servant dropped on his hair a little concentrated attar of roses, or burned sweet incense round his head for a moment. When a Rabbi came to visit he was always greeted by his host placing his right hand on the Rabbi's left shoulder and his left hand on the Rabbi's right shoulder and then kissing him. Jesus pointed out that not one of these acts of conventional courtesy had been offered to him, and that the woman, in her own way, had done what she could to supply them.

The Two Debtors

Then Jesus told a story. A creditor had two debtors. One owed him 500 denarii and the other 50. When both the debtors were quite unable to pay, the creditor graciously cancelled both debts. Which debtor, asked Jesus, will love the creditor most? Simon gave the obvious answer that the man who had been forgiven the greater debt will feel the greater love. Just so, said Jesus, this woman had great sins and the forgiveness of them has moved her to great love. Then Jesus, to the surprise and resentment of the other guests, told the woman that her sins were forgiven and bade her go in peace.

G

The Love of the Forgiven Heart

Does this parable teach that only one who has been forgiven great sins can feel a great love for Jesus? In one sense that is true. It is true that it is only when we discover what Jesus has done for us that we can really love him as we ought. John Oxenham has an imaginative reconstruction of what happened to Barabbas after the crowd chose him to be set free and so sent Jesus to the Cross. After the verdict Barabbas followed Jesus to Calvary to see what would happen. When the nails were driven through Jesus' hands, one thought was in Barabbas' mind. 'These nails should have been driven through my hands, not his—he saved me.' When he saw Jesus finally hanging on the Cross one feeling was in Barabbas' heart, 'I should have been hanging there, not he—he saved me.'

A missionary in India told the story of Jesus to a village which had never heard it before. After the story had been told in words, it was shown in pictures thrown on the side of a whitewashed house. They were watched in complete silence until there was one of Jesus on his Cross. Then a man in the audience suddenly sprang forward, 'Come down from that Cross, Son of God,' he shouted. 'That is my place, not yours.' One thing is clear about the death of Jesus. He suffered all he did for the sake of men; and had men not sinned against God, he would not have needed to suffer it. It follows that it was for our sakes he suffered and died, and when we see what he has done for us it should awaken our love for him.

The Man who needed no Forgiveness

It is just here that we arrive at the root difference between Simon the Pharisee and the woman. As Hugh Martin put it, 'The woman knew from what she had been saved. Simon, armoured in self-complacency, was not conscious that he needed saving from anything.' The woman was desperately conscious that she needed forgiveness; Simon was not.

One of the most grave mistakes we make is to identify sin with what we call the *grosser* sins. Anyone can see when an individual has been guilty of drunkenness, adultery or crime. But there are sins which no one can see except those who live with us; which cannot be punished by any law and yet which produce far more unhappiness for far more people over a far longer period—sometimes for a lifetime—than the sins of the hot heart. Sins like selfishness, meanness, sarcastic pride, the over-critical tongue, irritability and moodiness can wreck life for those we meet in the privacy of our own homes, and about them the world at large knows nothing. Simon was every bit as bad a sinner as the woman was, and perhaps much worse, but he did not know it; and because he did not know it, he did not feel the surge of love that she felt.

The lesson of the parable is that, only when we are conscious of our sins do we feel the love that we ought to feel for all that Jesus has done for us—and the wonder of being forgiven.

29

The Last State
of that Man is worse than the First

Matthew 12:43-45

Evil Spirits

SOMEONE has called this the Story of the Haunted House. At the back of it is the vivid Jewish belief in evil spirits. All the ancient world had this belief in spirits. They said that the atmosphere was so full of them that a pin could not be inserted into it without striking against one.

The Jews believed that these evil spirits originated from one of two sources. They might be the spirits of wicked people who had died but were still carrying on their malicious work. More commonly they were connected with the strange old story in Genesis 6:4, where we are told that the sons of God came to earth and begat children of the daughters of men. These children were supposed to be the unclean spirits who haunted the air. It is to such spirits Paul refers when he speaks of 'principalities and powers.'

The Work of the Spirits

All illness was ascribed to these spirits. The Egyptians believed there were 36 parts in the human body, and all of them might be presided over by a good or an evil spirit; and if an evil spirit was in charge, illness must follow. It was particularly easy to see in madness and epilepsy the work of evil spirits which occupied the bodies or the minds of men. There were certain special directions in which these spirits were given their chance. They were supposed to lurk when a man was eating and to get into his body along with the food. It was held to be specially true that they lurked in crumbs of food which had been left lying out. They were believed to lurk near unwashed hands and, if a person ate with unwashed hands, he was giving them a special chance to enter into him. They were believed to lurk in water drunk in a strange place or given by a stranger. The lonely places were their favourite abode. There was only one way to dispose of them and that was to drown them in deep water. We may remember how the healing of the Gadarene demoniac was proved to be complete because the swine into whom the evil spirits entered plunged into the sea.

Jesus and the Evil Spirits

Over and over again we read of Jesus healing people who had evil spirits and actually commanding them to come out. It has troubled many people that Jesus did this. They are of the opinion that belief in evil spirits was merely a superstition which men have long outgrown; and they wonder if Jesus shared in this superstition.

Dr Leslie Weatherhead deals with the problem of demon possession in his book, *Psychology, Religion and Healing*. There are various possible views. It may be held that Jesus was in scientific matters a child of his age and that frankly he knew no better. It may be held that Jesus was a wise psychologist and that, although he knew there were no evil spirits, he also knew that the spirits were very real to the people who believed themselves possessed by them; and therefore he treated them as real in order to cure the sufferer. Finally it may be held that evil spirits do exist.

It is impossible to hold that Jesus was merely ignorant and did not know any better. For one thing, it was not every sickness he attributed to evil spirits. And what is still more suggestive, he definitely did not share the common ideas of his time about evil spirits. Dr Weatherhead quotes a passage from a book by Dr William Menzies Alexander, a doctor of medicine:

[Jesus] commanded his disciples to gather up the fragments; thus discouraging the idea that demons lurk in crumbs. He had no faith in ceremonial washing of hands; so repelling the notion that spirits may rest on unwashed hands. He asked a draught of water from the woman of Samaria and thereafter entered the city; proving that he had no fear of drinking borrowed water and no belief in local *shedim*. He retired repeatedly to desert places and fasted

171

in the wilderness; therein rejecting the popular conception that the waste is the special haunt of evil spirits.

Quite clearly Jesus did not share the belief of his contemporaries in evil spirits; and yet he treated many sick people as if they were indeed possessed by them.

We may well then pose the question, 'Do these demons really exist?' Can perhaps, even yet, an illness which has no physical explanation can be explained by the action of evil spirits? We have no certain knowledge; but the fact remains that those who speak of this are not nearly so dogmatic as once they were, that possession by evil spirits is to be regarded only as an ancient and out-worn superstition.

The Story Jesus told

Jesus told of an evil spirit who had been ejected from the personality of a man. The spirit wandered about seeking rest. Then he came back. He found the man's personality swept and cleansed but empty. So he went and got seven spirits who were worse than himself and took over the empty personality again; and the last state of the man was far worse than the first. Here again Jesus is telling something which would be very vivid to his listening audience because empty houses were supposed to be the abode of demons and no one would enter a house which had long stood empty if he could possibly avoid it.

No Negative Goodness

What did Jesus mean by this weird story? He meant that it is no good cleansing an individual of evil things without putting good things in their place. It is not possible to leave a man's heart or mind empty. We must go on to put the good things in or the evil things will come back with more force than ever.

Jesus was thinking of the Pharisees. All their religion was built on the commandments which start, 'Thou shalt not ....' It was a religion of *not* doing things. It tried to empty men of all evil things but it did not tell them what the good things were. It is never enough to say, 'Thou shalt not .... ' and to stop there. Let us take a simple analogy. Suppose a man enters into possession of a garden which has run wild. He digs it, takes out the weeds and cleanses the whole place. But if he leaves it like that the weeds will come back and cover the soil again. He cannot leave it empty; he must go on to plant flowers; and in the end he must plant so many flowers that there is no room for weeds.

Let us see how this works in human nature. Take the case of an athlete. He or she does not drink or smoke, lives a clean, healthy life; and does so without any real difficulty. Why? Because the desire to excel as an athlete has quite thrown out of the mind the desire for self-indulgence. A person who had no athletic desires might well succumb to the temptations, because there was nothing else to put in their place. It is never enough to try to erect a good life on, 'Thou shalt not ....' We must not merely hate evil; we must love goodness.

Habits

This has some very practical consequences. It means that if we want to beat a bad habit the best way is to acquire a good one. Psychologists tell how our thoughts work. The substance of that part of the brain with which we think is soft. If we think a thought once it leaves an infinitesimal scratch; if we think the thought twice the scratch is deepened; and if we go on thinking that though, it literally runs in a groove and we cannot get it out. If we find a questionable interest gaining too strong a grip of our minds and lives, the way to conquer it is to acquire another interest which will be strong enough to drive it out.

Thoughts

This is particularly true of thoughts. Often we think the wrong things. If we say to ourselves, 'I will not think about this,' the only effect is to fix our thoughts upon it. The real way of escape is to think of other things, to plunge into other activities, to gain other interests. We cannot simply drive out badness; we must eject what is bad by the power of what is good. There is only one final way to do that. Paul said two great things. 'For me to live is Christ' (Philippians 1:21); and 'It is no longer I who live, but Christ who lives in me' (Galatians 2:20). What he meant was that his love for Jesus had driven the lesser things out. When we find ourselves giving such love and loyalty to Jesus that he comes first, we shall find that evil things have lost their power.

30

Which did the Will of his Father?
Matthew 21:28-32

A Very Human Story

THE Parable of the Two Sons is a very human story. There was a man who owned a vineyard. Work was required to be done in it. He had two sons and went to the first of them to request him to do a day's work in the vineyard. The son flatly and discourteously refused; but afterwards he changed his mind and went. The father went to the second son with the same request. He very politely said, 'Certainly I will go, sir,' but went away and did nothing about it. Jesus asked, 'Which of these two sons really did the will of his father?' And his bearers were bound to answer that the first one did in spite of his first refusal.

The Original Meaning

The original meaning is clear. The first son stands for the tax-collectors and the sinners. Their lives looked like a blunt refusal to have anything to do with God; and yet when Jesus came they listened to him and changed their lives to fit his message and meet his demands. The second son stands for the Scribes and the Pharisees. Their lives were one long profession that they would serve God and obey his commandments, and yet when the Son of God came they refused to have anything to do with him and in the end crucified him.

The parable occurs in the midst of an argument that Jesus was having with the chief priests and the elders of the people (Matthew 21:23) and in effect he is saying to them, 'All your lives you have been making a great profession of your devotion to God and now your attitude to me belies your whole profession. The people you brand as sinners have all their lives seemed to be turning their backs on God; but now they have changed their minds and have found a place in the Kingdom which you have thrown away.'

Words and Deeds

There is, however, far more than a local significance in this parable. It lays down the always valid truth that words can never take the place of deeds. There is a difference in the way the two sons answer their father's request. The first answers with almost contemptuous bluntness. The second says all the things which politeness demands, even adding 'sir' to his reply. But neither verbal courtesy nor surface politeness could take the place of deeds.

In the last analysis it is only by deeds that we really prove that we love someone. No doubt when we were children we had the experience of going to our mother and telling her we loved her, only to have her answer, 'Well, I wish you would show it a little more.' In ancient days the knights came to their ladies demanding the hardest tasks in order to prove their devotion.

The earliest title for Christianity was 'The Way' (*cf* Acts 9:2). It was never simply learning facts or reciting certain creeds. It was a way of life which proved its loyalty by its deeds.

A Curious Variant

It so happens that, although this may be crystal clear to us, it was a shock to the Jews. The New Testament manuscripts are full of variations on this parable; and many of them say that it was not the first son but the second who did his father's will. A quite common attitude of mind among the Jews is illustrated by J A Findlay with a modern example. He tells of a missionary in Palestine who told this story exactly as it is told in our version of the New Testament. He then put the question, 'Who did the will of his father?' To his great surprise the crowd unanimously answered, 'The man who said he would go and did not.' When they were asked why, they said, 'A day's work in the vineyard is a little thing, but to say 'No' to your father's beard is a grievous sin.' Such a verdict thinks that fair words are more important than fair deeds. The teaching of Jesus is precisely the opposite. He lays it down that profession can never be a substitute for performance.

It may be said that these two sons stand for two different kinds of people. Let us take the second first. He stands for those whose profession is worse than their practice. There have always been people whose words said one thing and whose lives said another. The classic example is Holy Willie, whom Burns pilloried forever in 'Holy Willie's Prayer' in which he makes him say:

O Thou wha in the heavens dost dwell,
Wha, as it pleases best thysel,
Sends ane to Heaven and ten to Hell
        A' for Thy glory,
And no for ony guid or ill
        They've done afore Thee!

I bless and praise thy matchless might
Whan thousands Thou hast left in night,
That I am here afore thy sight,
        For gifts an' grace
A burnin' an' a shinin' light,
        To a' this place.

Yet I am here a chosen sample,
To show thy grace is great and ample:
I'm here a pillar in thy temple,
        Strong as a rock,
A guide, a buckler and example
        To a' thy flock?

This man was William Fisher, farmer at Montgarswood, Ayrshire, and elder in the parish kirk at Mauchline. He professed to be a burning and a shining light; he set himself up as a judge of other people and as a pillar of the Kirk; and yet this same man was a drunken reprobate who used his position as 'The elder at the plate' to help himself to the church offerings, who seduced more than one country girl and who finally died in a ditch in a snowstorm on his drunken way home from Mauchline.

This kind of person does the greatest possible harm to the Church and to the cause of Christ. Preacher Dick Sheppard spent a great deal of his time speaking in the open air. Most of his audience were indifferent to Christianity and many were actively hostile. After he spoke he always undertook to answer questions and to enter into discussion, and after years of this he said that he had been forced to the conclusion that 'the greatest handicap the Church has is the unsatisfactory lives of professing Christians.' Everyone who has anything to do with any organisation of the Church, especially those who are professed members of the Church, is an advertisement for Christianity. If this life fits, or tries to fit, his profession, he is a good advertisement; if not, he is a bad debt to the Church.

Henry Drummond used to tell of speaking at a street corner to a group of young men who had no use for the Church. A man passed by and one of the young men said, 'That man is the founder of our Atheists' Club.' Drummond asked in astonishment, 'How can that be? He is one of the leading elders in the Church.' Back came the answer, 'Precisely! If a man who lives a life like that is one of its leading people, we want nothing to do with the Church.' It is an awe-inspiring thought that our lives every day either attract or repel people to Christianity according to our fidelity or lack of fidelity to our profession. Someone once said to a person who professed the finest things but did not live them, 'I cannot hear what you say for listening to what you are.' Those whose profession is contradicted by their practice do infinite harm to Christ and his Church.

Practice better than Profession

The strange thing is that it is quite possible for the reverse to be true. There are people like the first son whose practice is much better than their profession. There are people who insist that they make no kind of profession to Christianity and who yet live the finest of lives.

This confronts us with a very common problem. Over and over again it is stated that there are as good Christians outside the Church as there are inside. It is not possible to deny that there are good people outside the Church. No Christian man would want to deny it, for 'The true light … enlightens every man' (John 1:9).

· But let us take an analogy. Suppose a war is in progress. Suppose a man says, 'I am in complete sympathy with the aims of this war but I will not join the army. Rather I will carry on a war all by myself and will go out and fight the enemy all alone.' It is beyond doubt that practically all his effort and courage will be wasted; whereas if he joined with his fellow countrymen in common effort he would be of far more use. It is so with the Church. If we are on the side of Christ, then our place is in the ranks of Christ. It is by making common cause with the friends of Christ that we will be of most effect in the world.

There are many people, like the first son in the parable, whose practice is better than their profession; but they would be better still if they openly admitted where the loyalty of their hearts really lies.

Two Unsatisfactory People

The real root of the parable is in this—it is a story about two sons, neither of whom was fully satisfactory. True, the first was a better man than the second; but neither was perfect. It is better to say no and then go and obey, than it is to say yes and then go and disobey. But it is best of all to say yes with courage and then obey with fidelity. Both sons in the parable hurt their father's heart. The son who really brings joy to his father is the son who willingly hears and gladly obeys.

31

He Counteth the Cost
Luke 14:25-33

On counting the Cost

HERE Jesus uses two pictures to compel people to see that, before they follow him, they must count the cost. The first picture is of a man who wishes to build a tower. If he is wise he will carefully reckon up his resources before he starts in case he is not able to finish the building and so becomes a laughing stock. It may well be that the tower in question was a vineyard tower (Matthew 21:23). In a fully equipped vineyard there was always a tower from which watch was kept for the thieves who tried to rob the vineyard when the harvest was near. It is likely that Jesus took this picture from his own experience. He was for years the village carpenter of Nazareth. But in those days the carpenter was much more than a joiner. He was a mason and builder and everything else. The word that the New Testament uses for carpenter is *tekton*, which is almost the word *technician*. Very likely when Jesus was a carpenter he had experience of reckless men with grandiose schemes which they began but were never able to finish.

The other picture is of a king engaged upon a campaign. Before he starts out he will reckon up his chances against the odds arrayed against him, and only then will he go out to battle. If the odds are such that victory is impossible, he will come to terms rather than risk annihilation.

The Honesty of Jesus

If there is one thing that must strike us as we read the story of Jesus' appeal to men, it is his uncompromising honesty. No one could ever say that he had been induced to follow Jesus under false pretences. In Matthew 10, Jesus makes statement after statement which seems calculated to discourage rather than encourage men to follow him. In

Luke 9:57-62 when three men protested their willingness to follow him, he ordered each of them to count the cost. He laid down the terms of service in all their uncompromising demands and said to men, 'If you think you can face up to that, come; but count the cost in time.' That is what he is doing in this parable. He was on his way to Jerusalem and the crowds were surging round him. He knew well that most of them had quite the wrong idea about him. He knew that they had vague hopes that he would become a king and a conqueror. He wanted them to know the cost of following him.

Jesus counts the Cost

The parable has a curious double significance. First of all, it has *significance for Jesus himself.* If we look at it in one way, Jesus is the person who is building and the king who is on a campaign. He is in the world to build up the Kingdom of Heaven and to lead a campaign against the forces of evil. If his work is not to collapse about him, *he* needs men on whose loyalty he can depend. Unless he gets these men, *he* will be like the person who began to build and could not finish, or like the king who went on a campaign without reckoning up his own strength and the strength of his adversary.

Here we are face to face with God's method in this world. He works out his purposes through mankind. If he wants a task done he has to find some one willing to do it for him. If he wants a message taken to mankind, a great discovery made, a new truth told, a warning conveyed, he has to find some one to be his instrument. As someone put it, 'God is everywhere looking for hands to use.' Or, as someone else has said, 'The greatest thing about God is that he allows us to do so much for him.' Without irreverence we can say that God is as helpless without us as we are without him. It is he who supplies the vision and the power to carry out that vision; but he has to find men and women to whom to give the vision and the power.

There is an old legend which tells how Jesus, after his death and resurrection, returned to heaven. One of the angels met him and saw his wounds. The angel said, 'You must have suffered terribly down there in the world?' Jesus answered, 'I did.' 'Do all men know,' said the angel, 'how you loved them and suffered for them?' 'No, as yet only a few in a corner of Palestine know the story.' 'Well then,' said the angel, 'what have you done about letting all men know?' Jesus said, 'I have asked Peter and James and John and the rest to tell others, and the others to tell yet others and still others until the farthest man on the widest circle has heard the story.' The angel knew men and he was doubtful. 'Yes, but what if James and John and Peter forget? What if the rest fail in their task? What if the years go on and men do not tell others about you and your sacrifice? What then? Haven't you made other plans?' Back came Jesus' answer, 'I haven't made any other plans; *I'm counting on them.*' There we have the supreme honour which Jesus has given us. He depends on people to see to it that the building of the Kingdom which he began is brought to its completion, and that the campaign which he entered is brought to its triumphant conclusion. It is true that without him we can do nothing; but it is also true that without us his work cannot go on.

The Christian counts the Cost

Second, this parable *has significance for us:* that we must count the cost. Before we set out on the Christian way we must know what we are doing. That cost will be different for every person; but there are certain general laws which we can lay down.

(1) If a man sets out on the Christian way *it is the end of self.* He can no longer please himself; he must place himself entirely under the orders of Jesus Christ. It is told of Queen Elizabeth II that one day, when she was very young, she was forbidden to do something which she wanted to do. Like any child she was angry: 'I am a princess and I will do what I like,' she said. King George V, her grandfather, told her, 'My dear,' he said, 'you *are* a princess and that is the one reason why, all your life, you will never be able to do as you like.'

It is so with the Christian. The cost of following Christ is the abandonment of our own wishes and the complete acceptance of his. But this submission is not the broken submission of a slave to a master, or of a subject to a tyrant—it is the submission of love.

Abraham Lincoln once saw an African girl for sale in a slave market. He was always sorry for those held in slavery, but somehow the plight of this girl touched him deeply. He bought her and when she came to him, he handed her the papers of her freedom. He said to her, 'You are free now.' She looked at him with wondering eyes. 'Am I free?' she asked, 'free to go anywhere I like?' He said, 'Indeed you are.' 'Then, master,' she said, 'I will follow *you* forever.' Legally she was no longer a slave; but her heart had become the slave of love to him who had given her so much.

(2) If a man sets out on the Christian way, *it is the end of the world's scale of values.* In general the world assesses the value of a person by the material things he possesses or by the power he wields; Christianity assesses the value of a person by the amount he has given away and by the service he renders. The world's principle is that a person should live for himself; the Christian principle is that he or she should live for others.

If someone enters upon the Christian way, personal ambition must be abandoned and replaced by the ambition to be among mankind as one who serves.

(3) If a man sets out on the Christian way, there is *a new scale of loyalties.* He has set out on a life in which Christ comes first. In Luke 14:26 Jesus tells men that he who will follow him must hate his nearest and dearest. That is not to be taken literally; it is the normal eastern way of putting a truth as vividly as possible; but it does mean that loyalty to Christ must take precedence over all other loyalties.

It is a curious thing that the enemies of Christianity have seen that quite clearly. For instance, Hitler banished all professing Christians from his government because he said their loyalty to the state was endangered by their loyalty to Christianity. He knew quite well that, with a real Christian, if a clash of loyalties came, then Christ would come first. The reason is quite clear. It is that our relationship to Jesus Christ is a relationship of love and there is a certain exclusiveness in love. It is told of a great Scottish chieftain that, when he was confronted with the choice of death or of denying his loyalty to the Stuarts, his answer was, 'You can take my head from my shoulders but you will never take my heart from my king.' When we begin the Christian way, we must realise that Jesus Christ *must* have first place in our lives.

32

We are Servants

Luke 17:7-10

Man and God

JESUS takes a picture from everyday life. Suppose a master has a slave who has been out on the farm ploughing the land or tending the cattle. When that slave comes in, will the master tell him to sit down and eat? No, he will tell the slave to prepare a meal and to wait on him, and only after that will he himself be allowed to eat and drink. Surely, says Jesus, no master offers profuse thanks to a slave for doing what it is his ordinary duty to do. It is just so with us. When we have done our duty, we have earned no thanks for we have done only what we were bound to do.

The Revised Standard Version concludes the parable with the words, 'We are unworthy servants; we have only done what was our duty.' But some of the very earliest New Testament manuscripts omit the word 'unworthy,' and say simply, 'We are servants.' And that is the point. In regard to God, man is always a servant.

Trying to put God in our Debt

First and foremost Jesus teaches that we cannot ever put God in our debt. When we have done our utmost, we have still done only what we ought to do. This was a lesson that the orthodox Jews of the time badly needed to learn. They had a doctrine of works and believed in what we can only call a balance sheet morality. They thought of goodness in terms of credit and debit entries on a balance sheet; and they quite literally thought of the possibility of a man piling us a kind of credit account with God.

They believed there was a certain minimum obligation. If a man fulfilled that minimum, then he was all square with God. But, in addition, there were certain acts which a man might perform of his own free will and, if he did them, he had a kind of credit balance with God. They had a strange classification of men into three kinds. First, there were those who did a sufficient number of good works to be justified. They were the righteous. Second, there were those who did not. They were the wicked. And third, there was an intermediate class who were neither one nor the other, but who, by doing one extra good work, could pass into the class of the righteous. They saw all goodness as a kind of profit and loss account kept with God, and they believed it was quite possible for a man to put God in his debt.

That is a frame of mind which is not altogether absent today. A minister tells how he was talking to a man to whom life had been very kind and who had been highly successful. When leaving him he said, 'Well, God has been very good to you.' And the man answered, 'Yes, but I've been not bad to him.'

Surely if we were only to think of what God has done for us, we would know that it is not possible to put him in our debt. The reason is simply that God's relationship to us is a relationship of love. And it is impossible to pay for the gifts of love. Could, for instance, any gift, however generous, pay our parents for what they have done for us? Such a gift may show that we are grateful, but it can never discharge a debt which is beyond discharging. When we remember the gifts of God, crowned by the gift of his Son, then we can only say, in the words of Isaac Watts:

Were the whole realm of Nature mine,
  That were an offering far too small;
Love so amazing, so divine,
  Demands my soul, my life, my all.

The Insufficiency of Duty

Further, this parable teaches the insufficiency of mere duty. No one should feel that he has earned thanks for doing what in any event he could have been compelled to do. Take the case of a parent. The law does not lay down a reward for a parent who feeds, clothes and educates his or her child. But is does lay down a penalty for the parent

185

who does not. No one should expect any special praise for simply doing their duty. The person who is valued most is the one who goes beyond duty and beyond what the law lays down. The person who grimly follows duty, and determinedly stops when that duty has been done, will never get on in the world. It is the person who is willing to go the extra mile who gets somewhere in the end. Once again, when we apply this to ourselves and God, we are met with a situation in which there is no such thing as a completed duty. When we think of all that the love of God has done for us, it is impossible for us to say, 'I have done my duty: now I will stop,' for the simple reason that nothing we can do can ever discharge the debt we have to God. Love never thinks of service as a duty, but always as a privilege; and love's desire is not to do the irreducible minimum, but to give its all to the person whom it loves.

The Never-ending Task

Further, this parable shows that there are no set hours in the Christian life. A person cannot say, 'I will work for so many hours at being a Christian and then I will take time off.' All day and every day we must seek to follow our Master and to serve our God. One of our gravest faults is what we might call spasmodic goodness. For a time we really try to be good; and then we say to ourselves—perhaps unconsciously—'I will let up for a while and take things easy.' It was Milton who had the great thought that all life is lived in our great task-master's eye. There is no time for relaxation in the effort of the Christian life.

Master and Servant

It may well be that in the very characters of its story the parable lays down something which we would do well to remember. Jesus speaks of us and of God in terms of slaves and Master. The idea of God which is most dear to us is that of Father. But it is so easy to sentimentalise this idea and to think of God as an easy-going Father who does not greatly care what his children do.

186

When the German essayist Heine was dying, he was not in the least troubled. Asked why, he answered that he was sure God would forgive. Asked why he was so sure, he answered, 'It is his trade.' It is extremely easy to find an easy escape in the thought of God as Father. But Jesus was never afraid to speak of God as Master and ourselves as servants; and over the over again Paul uses as his proudest title for himself, the *servant* or the *slave of God*.

A father who really loves his child will be the last person to let that child do as he or she likes, without concern. He will be the first person to demand that discipline, that fidelity, that diligence which will enable the child to reach his full stature in the world. There is a famous Scottish family whose motto is 'Saved to serve.' We do well to think of God, not as a Father who lets his children do whatever they like, but as a Master who, having given his best to us, demands our best from us.

33

He that Humbleth Himself shall be Exalted
Luke 14:7-11

The Guests at the Feast

IT was actually at a feast that Jesus spoke this parable (Luke 14:1-6) and it may well be that he was describing something that actually happened. At a feast in Palestine the table was like a low solid block and round it were low couches on which the guests reclined. The table was arranged in the form of a 'U', like a square with one side unoccupied. In the centre of the top side sat the host. The first place of honour was at his right-hand side; the second place at his left-hand side; the third place was the second on the right; the fourth place was the second on the left, and so on around the table

Usually the exact hour of a feast was not specified. Those who were eager and grateful for the invitation usually came early, while those who had a good conceit of their own importance usually came late so that all could see their arrival. It was therefore very common for the people who were socially unimportant to be there early, and for the really important guests to arrive last. If then one of the early comers were to take one of the highest and most honourable places, the chances were that he would be asked to move when the honoured guests arrived. So Jesus' advice was that when a man was invited to a feast he should not set himself down in a place of honour lest he had the shame of being asked to move down to make way for someone more important. Rather he should take the lowest place he could find so that he might be invited to move up and so be honoured in the presence of his fellow guests.

Humility

Here then Jesus lays down the importance of *humility*. There are two realms in which humility is of supreme importance. It is important in the realm of knowledge. No one will ever begin to learn unless he realises that he does not know; therefore the first prerequisite of learning is the admission of one's ignorance. Again, humility is of supreme importance in the realm of the spirit. It has been said that the gateway to heaven is so low that no one can enter except upon their knees. The first essential of all religion is a sense of need. The person who is proudly self-sufficient cannot find God; the person who is humble enough to know his need will find the way open to God's presence.

Pathways to Humility

We will then do well to find the pathways that lead to humility.

(1) *Our very physical constitution should keep us humble.* We talk much these days about the powers which mankind has acquired and about the forces which he has harnessed. But surely the outstanding thing about man is his defencelessness. Not his strength, but his weakness, marks him out. Our human constitution is such that, though man be the crown of creation, a drop of water or a draught of air can kill him. When Alexander Pope, the famous poet, was dying, there was a time when he lost his reason. When he came to himself again and thought of his weakness and his humiliation, he whispered to a friend, 'I wonder now how there can be such a thing as human vanity.' The very fact that life's machinery can so easily break down, that life's strength so inevitably decays, that life's faculties grow so quickly blunted, should be enough to make a man realise his helplessness and to preserve him from pride.

(2) *The smallness of our achievements should keep us humble.* When the balance is struck there is really so little that anyone can claim to have done. Keats suggested as his own epitaph, 'Here lies one whose name was writ in water.' To him it seemed that he had left no mark on life. Even a man who did such great work as John Wesley, said at the end of his life, 'I can see nothing that will bear looking at.' It is not uncommon to find people taking a pride in the amount of work that they get through. But when we really come to think of it, what difference would it make to the life of the world if we were removed

tomorrow? No one is indispensable. Who among us will be remembered twenty years after we have passed from the world? For every man or woman who will be remembered, hundreds of thousands will be forgotten. The insignificance of our achievement ought to keep us from pride.

(3) *The smallness of our knowledge should keep us humble.* There has never been one great scholar who was impressed by the amount of knowledge he or she had acquired. Always the really great scholars have been humbled by the thought of the wide areas of human knowledge of which they knew nothing. It is one of the curious paradoxes of learning that the more we learn about any subject, the more we realise we have yet to learn. In the Academy at Athens, where the flower of Greek youth came to study, there was a three year course. In the first year the youths were called 'the wise men.' In their second year they were called 'those who loved wisdom.' But in their final year they were simply called 'the learners.' The further they proceeded into knowledge the more they realised how little they knew. We may easily realise this for ourselves. A person may be an expert in foreign languages and yet be so handless that mending an electric fuse proves impossible. Someone else may be learned in philosophy and yet quite unable to cook a meal. Another may be an expert in all kinds of machinery and yet know none of the world's hundreds of languages but his own, and may not even know that very well. Of all incomprehensible things intellectual pride is the most incomprehensible. Any thinking person must find his own ignorance far more staggering than any knowledge he may possess.

(4) *The fact that we have so little goodness should keep us humble.* Here the supremely important thing is the standard against which we measure ourselves. If we measures ourself against a low standard, we may be well pleased with ourself. And that is precisely what many people do. They claim that they are as good as their neighbours. No doubt they are, but that is not the point. The Christian comparison is with the goodness of God as revealed in the life of Jesus; and when we compare ourselves with that, there is nothing left to say except what Peter said when he realised who Jesus was, 'Depart from me, for I am a sinful man, O Lord' (Luke 5:8). If ever

we feel pride in our own goodness, a moment's comparison with the life of Jesus will reduce us to the humility we ought to have.

Our Self-valuation

There is another suggestive point in this parable. It asks the question —does your own judgment of your worth coincide with the judgment of your fellow men? The man who took the highest place uninvited set a considerable value upon his worth; but it was a judgment which was not endorsed by his fellows. The judgment of our fellow men is not to be despised. Men instinctively admire honour and honesty, generosity and kindness, straightness and fidelity, the humble and the self-effacing spirit. Burns was right when he wrote:

O wad some Pow'r the giftie gie us
To see oursels as ithers see us!
It wad fae monie a blunder free us,
    An' foolish notion:
What airs in dress an' gait wad lea'e us,
    An' ev'n devotion!

It would often be a salutary experience to know what others are thinking of us.

34

Founded upon a Rock

Matthew 7:24-27; Luke 6:46-49

The House and its Foundation

IT is fitting that we should end our study of the parables with that one which above all lays down the claim of Jesus to be the only guide for life. The versions of Matthew and Luke are slightly different but the essential meaning is the same. The difference comes from the fact that the gospel according to St Matthew was written by a Jew who knew intimately the conditions of life in Palestine; while the gospel according to St Luke was written by a Greek who put the story in more universal terms which would be understood in any land.

In Matthew, the point is the place where the man chose to build. In Palestine, a place which might be a raging river in autumn was a dry gully in summer. In the summertime a foolish builder might find a pleasantly sheltered hollow, where the ground was smooth and level and, without thinking, might proceed to build there. But the autumn rains would come with their torrential downpour, the sheltered gully would become the bed of a raging torrent and the foolish builder would see his house swept away. But the wise builder would know better. He would know well that a place which in summer looked seductively sheltered would be in winter flooded with the swelling streams, and so he looked for a rock which would stand above the flood. He built on the rock, and when the storms came his house was safe. That was characteristically a Palestinian picture.

In Luke, the point is much more universal. The contrast is between a foolish builder who would not take the trouble to lay a proper foundation for his house but simply erected a jerry-built contraption sitting on the ground, and a wise builder who went to the labour of digging deep until he came to the sub-stratum of rock and laid the foundations there. When the storms came, the house of the foolish builder collapsed because it had nothing solid to rest on; but the house of the wise builder stood fast because the storms were powerless to move what was founded on the rock.

In essence the two pictures are the same. Remember that Jesus was in all probability much more than a carpenter. He would know all about building houses, because he had built them. As he so often did, he is taking a picture from his own experience to lead men to God.

The Tremendous Claim

In this parable Jesus is making a staggering claim. In effect he is saying that obedience to his teaching is the only safe foundation for life. He is saying that unless a man takes him as master, he cannot look for anything else but the ruin of his life. In anyone else a claim like that would be regarded as megalomaniac egotism. Other teachers make appeals, give advice, offer counsel; but Jesus presents men with an imperious demand. There is no coming to terms with Jesus; in Christianity there is no half-way house. The only agreement that one can make with Jesus is the agreement of complete submission.

It is told that Horatio Nelson was famous for his courtesy to his defeated enemies. On one occasion a defeated captain came onto Nelson's quarter-deck as a prisoner. He had heard of Nelson's courtesy and came forward holding out his hand almost as if he were at a reception. Nelson said, 'Your sword first—and then your hand.' The first necessity was submission. This parable teaches clearly that the claim of Christ must either be totally accepted or totally rejected. It is the claim of Jesus that to take his way is the way to security; to refuse to take it is the way to disaster.

Hearing and Doing

The implicit threat of the parable is against those who hear what Jesus has to say, but who never get beyond that hearing and turn it into action. That is a state in which the vast majority of people find themselves. Let us see if we can find some of the reasons why people listen to the commands of Jesus and fail to act on them although they know perfectly well that they ought to.

One of the most common reasons is reluctance to act *at once*. The psychologists tell us that one of the most dangerous things in life is repeatedly to feel an emotion and never to translate it into action. The more often we feel and fail to act, the less likely it is that we ever will. That is the supreme danger of listening to preaching and of worshipping in the house of God. Under the influence of the preacher and of the spirit of worship, we may feel moved to higher things; we may have the conviction that the life we are living will not do and that we must do better. But if all this remains at the stage of feeling and never translates itself into action, in the end it only hardens the heart.

Emotion can never be a substitute for action. There is a story of a Russian aristocrat lady in the old days, who was in a theatre watching an intensely moving play and weeping as she watched. Outside, her coachman was slowly freezing to death on the box of her coach, which he had been forbidden to leave until she emerged from the theatre. That lady was substituting emotion for action. In the theatre she wallowed in sentimental tears. Outside there was an opportunity to put that compassion into action; and she was not even aware of the opportunity.

How then shall we escape this danger of unconsciously substituting mere emotion for action? In the end there is only one way—by acting on our emotion at once. Any writer will say that the hardest sentence of any book to write is the first. He may sit for long enough looking at the blank page unwilling to make a start; but once he has penned that first sentence, the others will follow in a stream. Life is very much like that. The initial step is the hard step.

If, when we listen to the gospel of Jesus Christ, we have the feeling that we ought to help someone, to be less selfish, to be of more service, to rid ourselves of something evil, we should go straight out and translate that emotion into practical action. If we do not do it at once, the chances are that we will never do it at all. We endanger our very souls if again and again we hear the proclamation of the gospel and do nothing to translate the emotion produced into answering action.

The Long View

Another reason for not translating our hearing into doing is our almost chronic inability to take the long view. In Matthew's story, the foolish builder had not the sense to look into the future. All that was in his mind was that the spot where he proposed to build looked at the moment an entirely pleasant place. Had he allowed his mind to travel a few months ahead, he would have seen beyond doubt that he was building not for pleasure but for disaster. All through life we are constantly confronted with a choice between two goods—that which is good for the moment, and that which for the moment maybe difficult and demanding, but which is good in the long run. It is doubtless, for example, more pleasant to play games or enjoy amusements than to study; but when the months have passed and the examination has to be faced, it is not so pleasant then. The world is full of people who regret with all their hearts that they did not bear the yoke when they were young.

What is true of practical things is true also of the things of the spirit. In the last analysis there is only one test of any course of action. Not 'How does this look at the moment?', but 'How will this look in the sight of God?' There is a phrase which tells us to look at things *sub specie aeternitatis*, which means as they appear in the light of eternity. It is the height of folly to barter the values of eternity for the values of the passing moment. If we took the long view,we would follow our hearing with immediate doing.

Refusing to take the Trouble

Still another reason for failing to turn our hearing into doing is that we will not take the trouble. To set out on the Christian way demands an effort and we are unwilling to make it. In regard to this quite natural reaction we must remember two things. First, as someone has said, 'Jesus Christ came not to make life easy but to make men great.' The Christian way offers not ease but glory. Second, the hardness of the way will be forgotten in the glory of the journey's end. The athlete may find the days of training hard, but all the rigour is forgotten in the moment of victory. The student may find the days of study hard, but all the weariness of the discipline is forgotten in the day of achievement.

Robert Browning, in his poem 'Easter-day', tells of a tablet on the wall which recounts the history of one of the early martyrs:

I was born sickly, poor and mean,
A slave: no misery could screen
The holders of the pearl of price
From Caesar's envy; therefore twice
I fought with beasts, and three times saw
My children suffer by his law;
At last my own release was earned;
I was some time in being burned,
But at the close a Hand came through
The fire above my head, and drew
My soul to Christ whom now I see.
Sergius, a brother, writes for me
This testimony on the wall—
For me, I have forgot it all.

In the greatness of the prize, the effort of the way was quite forgotten. In this we have the example of Jesus himself who, as the writer of the letter to the Hebrews says, 'for the joy that was set before him endured the cross, despising the shame' (Hebrews 12:2). The Christian way demands an effort. But there is no joy like the joy of achievement; and we can be very sure that in the end the prize will be worth the cost. 'Be doers of the word, and not hearers only' (James 1:22).

At the end of our study of the parable we may well go out with that commandment in our minds. John Drinkwater, in his poem 'A Prayer', expressed it like this:

Grant us the will to fashion as we feel,
Grant us the strength to labour as we know,
Grant us the purpose, ribbed and edged with steel,
To strike the blow.

Knowledge we ask not, knowledge Thou hast lent,
But, Lord, the will—there lies our bitter need,
Give us to build above the deep intent
The deed, the deed.

Bibliography

Bruce, A B: *The Parabolic Teaching of Christ.*
Buttrick, G A: *The Parables of Jesus.*
Cadoux, A T: *The Parables of Jesus.*
Calderwood, H: *The Parables of our Lord.*
*Dodd, C H: *The Parables of the Kingdom* (Fount).
Dods, M: *The Parables of our Lord: First and Second Series.*
Findlay, J Alexander: *Jesus and his Parables.*
Goebel, S: *The Parables of Jesus.*
Hunter, A M: *Interpreting the Parables.*
*Jeremias, J: *The Parables of Jesus* (SCM Press).
Levison, N: *The Parables, their Background and Local Setting.*
*Linneman, E: *Parables of Jesus. Introduction and Exposition* (SPCK).
Luccock, H E: *Studies in the Parables of Jesus.*
M'Fadyen, J F: *The Message of the Parables.*
Martin, H: *The Parables of Jesus.*
Oesterley, W E O: *The Gospel Parables in the light of their Jewish
    Background.*
Roberts, R E: *The Message of the Parables.*
Shafto, G R H: *The Lesser Parables of Jesus.*
Smith, B T D: *The Parables of the Synoptic Gospels.*
Swete, H B: *The Parables of the Kingdom.*
Trench, R C: *Notes on the Parables of our Lord.*
Wilkinson, J: *Many things in Parables.*

* Denotes publication is still in print at time of press.